PUB WALKS ALONG

The Peddars Way and the Norfolk Coast Path

PUB WALKS ALONG
The Peddars Way and the Norfolk Coast Path

TWENTY CIRCULAR WALKS

Liz Moynihan

COUNTRYSIDE BOOKS
NEWBURY, BERKSHIRE

First published 1997
© Liz Moynihan 1997
This new edition 2004

COUNTRYSIDE BOOKS
3 Catherine Road
Newbury, Berkshire

ISBN 1 85306 861 6

To Bodger

Designed by Graham Whiteman
Cover picture of Weybourne supplied by Derek Forss
Photographs by Fergus Moynihan

Produced through MRM Associates Ltd., Reading
Printed and bound by J W Arrowsmith Ltd., Bristol

Contents

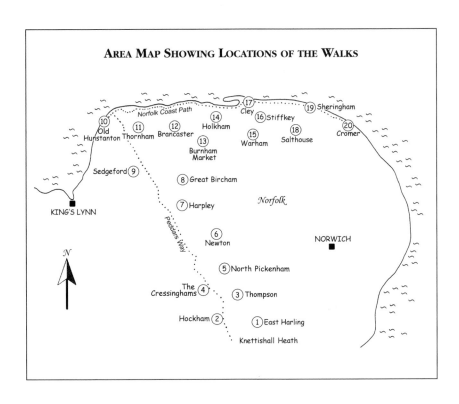

AREA MAP SHOWING LOCATIONS OF THE WALKS

Norfolk Coast Path

⑰ Cley

⑲ Sheringham

⑩ Old Hunstanton

⑪ Thornham

⑫ Brancaster

⑭ Holkham

⑯ Stiffkey

⑳ Cromer

⑬ Burnham Market

⑮ Warham

⑱ Salthouse

Sedgeford ⑨

Norfolk

KING'S LYNN

⑧ Great Bircham

⑦ Harpley

Peddars Way

⑥ Newton

NORWICH

⑤ North Pickenham

The Cressinghams ④

③ Thompson

Hockham ②

① East Harling

Knettishall Heath

N

Key for Maps

· · · · ·   Peddars Way and Norfolk Coast Path

→ · · · →   Pub Walk incorporating the long-distance path

Walk

Publisher's Note

We hope that you obtain considerable enjoyment from this book; great care has been taken in its preparation. However, changes of landlord and actual closures are sadly not uncommon. Likewise, although at the time of publication all routes followed public rights of way or permitted paths, diversion orders can be made and permissions withdrawn.

We cannot of course be held responsible for such diversion orders and any inaccuracies in the text which result from these or any other changes to the routes nor any damage which might result from walkers trespassing on private property. We are anxious though that all details covering the walks and the pubs are kept up to date and would therefore welcome information from readers which would be relevant to future editions.

INTRODUCTION

The Peddars Way and the Norfolk Coast Path (opened in 1986) are two totally different National Trails that together form a 93 mile route of astounding diversity through the best of Norfolk's scenery. The Peddars Way was a pre-historic trade route which was upgraded by the Romans at the time of their fight against Boudicca, queen of the Iceni tribe, into a route for moving troops rapidly through the countryside. Today it begins at Knettishall Heath just over the border in Suffolk. The Angles Way from Great Yarmouth terminates here, and this together with the linking route of the Weaver's Way from Cromer to Great Yarmouth, plus the Peddars Way and the Coast Path, make a route around Norfolk of 226 miles. The Icknield Way, starting from Ivinghoe Beacon in Buckinghamshire, also comes to Knettishall Heath. The Peddars Way, which has links with many other ancient routes running near or across its path, heads in very much of a straight line to Holme-next-the-Sea in Norfolk from where a ferry once plied across the Wash on a direct route into Lincolnshire. The importance of the Peddars Way is indicated by the fact that parts of it run along a built-up embankment (agger).

The Coast Path, by contrast, is a modern invention which takes advantage of old drove roads, smugglers' routes, cliff-top and marsh-side paths, to make a varied walking route starting at Hunstanton, two miles west of Holme, and following coastal or hillside paths to Cromer. The Coast Path in some places goes near beaches, or alongside creeks and marshes which can become underwater at high tides. Spring tides and following winds can sometimes bring the sea up even further. Always take care and check the state of the tide. It can also mean that some paths get very muddy under foot.

Be prepared, especially in high summer, for parts of the circular walks to be overgrown with weeds and sometimes brambles. It is wise to wear long trousers and long-sleeved shirts, and boots are recommended for ground which can be uneven or soggy.

The routes of these pub walks have been designed to show the amazing variety of scenery which Norfolk offers and to give some insight into the history and wildlife of the different areas. The pubs are equally diverse and interesting, some providing simple but welcome sustenance and others, gourmet treats. It is worth phoning first to check details especially if your party is large. Please don't use their car parks unless you are also using the pub and do leave a note on the dashboard explaining your plans. Many of the pubs are near or actually

Holme Dunes Nature Reserve on the Coast Path

on the Long Distance Routes but parts of the Peddars Way are very remote and in some cases a longer walk will be necessary to incorporate the nearest pub. Short cuts are indicated wherever possible. The book thus offers a choice of shorter or longer walks, an excellent variety of pubs and the possibility of linking each walk into the Long Distance Routes. The two routes can then be followed in one fell swoop on several consecutive days or tackled in bite-sized chunks over a longer period of time.

Simple sketch maps have been provided to give a guide to the circular walks and the links which make up the Long Distance Routes, but it is recommended that they are used in conjunction with the relevant Ordnance Survey maps, details of which are given in the preamble to each walk. Neither the Peddars Way nor the Coast Path has a special logo apart from the acorn sign which denotes a Long Distance Route. Signposting, which is not always consistent or helpful, can be by way of wooden signposts or plastic arrow markers.

Much of the two Long Distance Routes, especially the Coast Path, runs near nature reserves, Areas of Outstanding Natural Beauty (AONBs) or Sites of Special Scientific Interest (SSSIs), altogether making a popular destination where too many cars can create a nuisance at peak times.

The bus service along the coast has been greatly improved and could be a good and hassle-free means of reaching the walks. Trains run between Norwich and Cromer, and to Thetford within reach of Knettishall Heath. For specific bus and train information telephone: FREECALL 0500 626116.

For those who wish to tackle the whole route, the starting point of the Peddars Way lies on the western boundary of Knettishall Heath just over the border into Suffolk. A small road from the A1088 near Euston via Rushford to Hopton runs through this country park and gives easy access to the Way. There is car parking just over the road from the starting point where the Icknield Way terminates. Leave the road and go through a gate with a Peddars Way information board on the right and an acorn – the Long Distance Route waymark. Continue through woodland, then bear right and cross a bridge over the river Little Ouse into Norfolk. Continue on for a short distance and then bear left along a tree-lined path. Cross the A1066 and then a smaller road leading to East Harling. Soon after this is the route of the first walk.

Now all you have to do is to go out and enjoy yourself!

Liz Moynihan

EAST HARLING AND THETFORD FOREST

The Nag's Head

The typical Breckland village of East Harling with its splendid 15th century church in a lovely setting near the banks of the river Thet is the start of this varied walk. The route passes through the former settlements of West Harling, Middle Harling and Harling Thorpe, which were all virtually deserted by 1735. West Harling's atmospheric church, surrounded by fields and woodland, still survives. The final part of the walk is through Thetford Forest Park where the varied habitats of mixed woodland, pine trees and open heathland create a haven for wildlife.

East Harling is in the heart of Breckland – a vast area of sandy heathland and forests, interspersed with fields of wheat or sugar beet, mixed with free range pig production. Breckland was famous for its rabbit warrens in medieval times (rabbits farmed for the table). This and overgrazing by

11

sheep caused soil erosion which contributed to people moving from the villages. The splendid church of St Peter and St Paul has a stately 14th century tower and spire emerging from flying buttresses. Inside is a rare 15th century east window, ancient carved screens, some original choir stalls, a hammerbeam roof supported by angels and some wonderful monuments. The walk starts in the small village square opposite the Nag's Head pub. Just a few doors down is another old coaching inn – the Swan – which more than half a century ago was the home of a rich wool merchant. The nearby town of Thetford with its museums, ruins and the lovely Little Ouse river, has been an important town since the 9th century when the conquering Danes made it their capital.

Taking up almost the whole of one side of a small square of shops and houses in the large village of East Harling near Thetford is the Nag's Head. This friendly successful pub has made a name for itself with its food. There is a well-chosen bar menu, with specials that change every Friday. In addition, once a month there are two evenings of special themed food from different countries.

To complement the good food there is quite an extensive wine list. The pub is a freehouse and offers Adnam's Best and changing guest ales. Lagers are Stella Artois and Carlsberg and two draught ciders are available – Strongbow and Aspall. There is also Guinness and Calder's Irish beer. Hours for drinking are from 11.30 am to 3 pm and from 5 pm to 11.30 pm while food is served from 11.30 am to 2.30 pm and from 5 pm to 9 pm. On Saturday and Sunday the pub is open all day.

In the front of the pub a small lounge bar is decorated with regimental belt buckles and shields. There is a special games room and a restaurant at the back which opens onto a patio decorated with colourful flowers in summer for al fresco eating and drinking. There are smoking and non-smoking areas in the restaurant. The pub has four bed-and-breakfast rooms. Dogs are allowed in the garden. The pub is popular not only with locals but with families and walkers having holidays or days out in nearby Thetford Forest. Telephone: 01953 718140.

- **HOW TO GET THERE:** East Harling is about 8 miles east of Thetford on the B1111 which runs between the A11 and the A1066 at Garboldisham. The Nag's Head is on the main road in the centre of East Harling.
- **PARKING:** In the square or the car park of the Nag's Head, at the rear, entered from School Lane. Parking is also possible at Bridgham Lane or at

Thorpe Farm (signposted), both off the road running from the A1066 to East Harling.

• **LENGTH OF THE WALK:** 8 miles (with an opportunity for a short cut). Map: OS Explorer 230 Diss and Harleston (GR 994864).

THE WALK

1. Turn left out of the pub, passing the Swan Inn. At a junction of roads on a bend, follow the main road as it bends to the left and walk to the next junction. The church of St Peter and St Paul is a short detour away. Turn left along West Harling Road, signposted to Brettenham. After leaving the outlying houses of East Harling, the road passes through open farmland, then the few remaining buildings of Middle Harling with its green edged with old trees.

2. When the road bends sharply left, carry ahead onto a drive leading past a lodge on the right (a sign says Berdewelle Hall Farm), then through fenced fields. Near a garden wall and then a house on the left, bear half left along an narrow path through a few trees.

The splendid 15th century church of St Peter and St Paul, West Harling

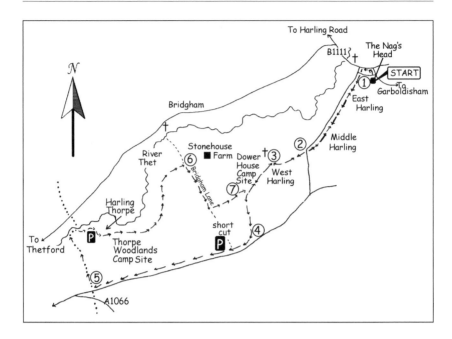

3. Soon turn left along a broad cross track, passing West Harling church over the field on the right, to reach another crossroads of tracks. Walk on ahead into woodland following a wide track which curves through the forest before coming out at another junction of paths. Ignore the path to the left and also the well used drive to the right leading to the Dower House camping site, and go straight ahead down another part of the drive which curves gently through beautifully scented woodland before passing a lodge on the left.

4. Just before the drive meets the main road turn right onto an overgrown woodland ride passing a bank (for stopping cars) and continue on to Bridgham Lane (a broad sandy drive) used as a picnic place and for parking. Avoid all other forest rides. For a short cut, turn right up this and continue the walk at stage 6. For the main walk carry on ahead over Bridgham Lane along the woodland ride for about a mile avoiding all cross tracks, to reach a small lane which leads to Thorpe Woodlands camp site and Forest Enterprise parking. Cross over the lane and continue on to Peddars Way.

 5. Turn right up Peddars Way which here is a gentle track

East Harling church

bounded by some mixed trees with views into fields on the left. There are signs of the aggar or embankment along which the Way would originally have run, indicating its importance. Pass through an area of common and continue on avoiding all side paths to reach the River Thet.

Turn right along the bank (the posts mark a woodland walk) along a boarded walkway. Peddars Way eventually turns left over the river. At this point, the walk leaves Peddars Way and carries on along the river, arriving shortly at a strip of woodland where it turns right into a camping field by Thorpe Farm. Continue up the edge of the field and bear left onto a short stretch of track which comes out at the farmhouse. Ignore the lane on the right which leads to the camp site from the road and bear left in front of the farmhouse (derelict). Ignore the first barred track leading to a camping field and take the next track left, continuing along a wide track (red topped marker posts). When this track or small road bears left to a house near the remains of Harling Thorpe church, continue ahead along a narrow track through woodland. This comes out onto a broad green track – the red topped posts mark a woodland trail.

Keep generally ahead, ignoring all side tracks, following the curves of the path for about a mile and a half through cleared patches and young trees amidst more mature stands. Emerge onto Bridgham Lane again near the track to Stonehouse Farm.

6. Turn right and walk along this wide sandy track through the forest. Ignore a ride to the right and carry on to a broad cross track with barriers. Turn left and walk along a broad grassy ride first through woodland, then a cleared area. At a cross track at an oblique angle near a bridleway sign, turn left and at the next cross track go straight over onto a path through woodland which comes out onto the drive to the Dower House camp site again.

7. Turn right along this to return to the junction of paths encountered on the outward journey. Turning left off the drive, retrace the route away from the forest, passing West Harling church again, turning right onto the path and drive leading back to West Harling road. Go back up the road, turning right to the pub.

   THE PEDDARS WAY – River Thet to Wretham (4 miles)

Cross the bridge over the River Thet and follow the path as it crosses the Brettenham to Bridgham road. Continue on through open countryside and belts of trees, then go alongside conifer woods on the right with Brettenham Heath (a remnant of old Breckland) on the left. Cross a small road and then the busy A11 Thetford to Norwich road taking great care. More care is needed at the level crossing over the railway. A track coming in from the left is Harling Drove, an important pre-Roman way passing through East Wretham and Roudham Heaths (Norfolk Wildlife Trust nature reserves). Continue on through woods and by the arches of an old railway bridge, bearing left then right to eventually reach the route of the next walk just before the A1075 road passing through Wretham.

HOCKHAM AND EAST WRETHAM
The Red Lion

The typical scenery of old Breckland with its patches of heather, grass and bracken, dotted with birch and hawthorn scrub as well as the more recent forest cover are both encountered on this walk through Thetford Forest Park near Great Hockham. On a hot summer's day the smell of the pines is superb. Several excellent nature reserves (including East Wretham Heath with its two meres and ancient Scots Pine plantation, Roudham Heath and Wayland Wood) lie near at hand and are well worth visiting while you are in the area.

Caston is an interesting village in the middle of Breckland, not far from Wayland Wood which is a remnant of ancient woodland managed by the Norfolk Wildlife Trust. It was here, as legend tells, that the Babes in the Wood met their sad fate. On Caston green stands the base of a late 15th century market or pilgrim's cross, possibly linked with early 16th century Church Farm, which was thought to have been a refectory for medieval pilgrims en route for Castle Acre and Walsingham. Opposite Church Farm is 14th century Holy Cross church, with its hammerbeam roof and glorious west window. A Victorian windmill stands out on the Watton road.

Next to the green in Caston stands the Red Lion, pretty with its flint and pantiled exterior. This cheerful village pub is painted a warm red inside with a red carpet in the dining room, and promises 'a roaring welcome'! Its menu varies from burgers, through a selection of six Indian dishes to steaks and more complicated dishes such as blanquette of lamb or leek or partridge in red wine gravy. There is a good choice of fish dishes and five vegetarian options. The changing menu is written up on boards. The pub keeps Adnam's ales and a changing guest beer as well as a choice of draught lagers and Guinness.

Opening hours are: 12 noon to 3 pm and 6 to 11 pm Monday to Thursday, Friday 12 noon to 2.30 pm and 5 to 11 pm. On Saturday and Sunday the pub is open all day from 12 noon to 11 pm (10.30 pm on Sunday). Food is served any time during lunch time opening and from 6 to 9 pm in the evening. Telephone: 01953 488236. From Caston it is a reasonably short drive to the beginning of the walk, which is the Hockham picnic and information area signposted off the A1075.

- **HOW TO GET THERE:** Caston is signposted off the A1075 south of Watton. Follow the road through Griston and on to Caston. To reach the parking place return to the A1075 and carry on further south. The Thetford Forest Park parking area (Hockham picnic site) is signposted off the A1075 roughly half way between Wretham (Stonebridge) and Great Hockham.
- **PARKING:** Plenty of parking at the forest parking place and at the pub.
- **LENGTH OF THE WALK:** 5½ miles (short cut available). Map: OS Explorer 237 Norwich (GR 938920).

THE WALK

1. Walk away from the road and parking area past a yellow striped barrier along a broad, sandy forest ride with a clearing on the right. Pass green/yellow posts indicating walks. Ignore a track to the right with a green topped marker post. Continue on passing a yellow topped post. Soon, at a T-junction of paths, turn left along a smaller path (the track to the right is quite wide). After a fairly short distance, go through by a barrier and cross the A1075 (footpath markers either side) which offers a short cut back to Wretham (Stonebridge).

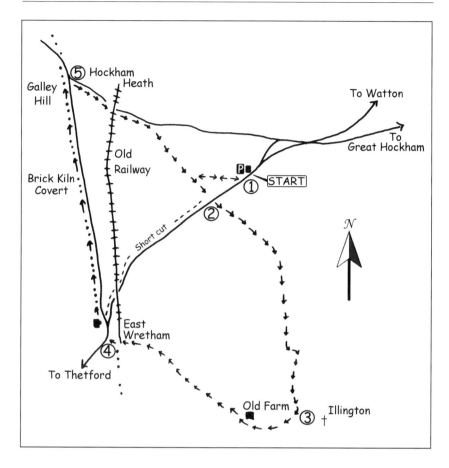

2. Pass another barrier and continue on along a wide track, going straight over a cross track. After some distance, cross another track and eventually come out onto a broad track near open fields. A marked bridleway goes off to the left, another path goes immediately right, but ignore these and go towards the right, down the broad track. At another junction of paths where a marked bridleway goes right and another track left, keep straight on alongside the woods. The track bears left so go with it, ignoring a broad ride to the right, and then soon bear right.

3. The path leaves the woods and passes through fields. Just where the track bends left to pass a shed, a footpath signpost points to the right along a track which bears right again passing woods on the left.

Thetford Forest

Bear left round a fishing pond, over a bridge and right along a narrow path to cross another little bridge (rather rank undergrowth). Look out for a small track bearing left away from the pond and passing under telephone wires into a field.

The right of way goes straight across the field and continues ahead through weedy undergrowth towards Old Farm, skirting along its garden wall (there is an arrow marker on the post just here). Pass the garden of the farm on the right. Another arrow marker by a gate here points to the left down a good track, past barns on the right. Ignore the drive which sweeps back into the farm and keep bearing right round the barns. At the end of the buildings there is an arrow marker on a post on the right not far from an open barn. Go a short distance along a good track to a field edge and then at an arrow marker almost hidden by nettles, bear left through the middle of a field (track just visible when I walked). Go through a hedgerow into another field (signpost on left). Go ahead through this field passing a copse over on the right and come to another footpath signpost at the field boundary. Continue ahead along a broad track alongside a huge field housing freerange pigs. At the end of the field go ahead over a piece of wasteland (footpath signpost) and come out onto the route of the Peddars Way by a variety of arrow markers.

 4. Bear right through the brick bases of an old bridge onto another track near houses (look for arrow markers) and bear right along the track through scattered housing to meet the A1075 (wooden signpost). Cross over. Take a small lane to the left signposted the Peddars Way. There are some large houses on the right and then the lane passes through farmland with scattered cottages and farms backed by woodland.

5. Coming to a road junction, leave the Peddars Way, which carries on bearing slightly left, and turn right. There is a footpath signpost on the grassy triangle here signposting the Long Distance Route and also the Pingo Trail (see Thompson walk) which turns onto the Peddars Way here. Ignore the access route into the forest (Hockham Heath) on the left and continue sharp right down a tiny lane through the middle of the forest. Ignore a footpath going off to the left and continue on over a bridge crossing the route of the dismantled railway. The road bends gently to the left near a cottage almost hidden in woods on the left. Soon after this a bridleway crosses the road. Turn right along this broad ride (marked by a Forestry Commission number and a bridleway signpost) passing a yellow striped barrier. Pass a yellow-topped post denoting forest walks. Ignore a path to the right and pass another yellow-topped post. To reach the parking place, bear left along the main path (yellow topped post) and retrace your steps.

THE PEDDARS WAY – Galley Hill to Thompson Water (1½ miles)

At Galley Hill, the Peddars Way changes direction (the only major change in its whole length) and continues by following a metalled road which soon bears left into the Stanford Battle Ground. Here the Peddars Way carries on as a stony track, passing through woods to reach Thompson Water.

THOMPSON AND THE PINGO TRAIL
The Chequers
❦

This delightful route meanders through woodland and open grassland grazed by Shetland ponies, passing pingos (shallow ponds formed at the end of the last Ice Age) - the habitat for a range of unusual wetland flora and fauna. They lend their name to the Great Eastern Pingo Trail (car park at Stow Bredon on the A1075), which forms part of this walk as it passes through Thompson Common Nature Reserve. Near Peddars Way lies the scenic expanse of Thompson Water, a shallow 40 acre lake owned by the Norfolk Wildlife Trust. Please note - no dogs are allowed on the reserve.

Thompson itself is a scattered village. The walk passes the splendid 14th century St Martin's church and its nearby knot of attractive cottages near the site of the college (or association of priests) attached to the church, funded by the Shardelowe family (lords of the manor, in 1200). The church is in the Decorated style with a 17th century box pew and pulpit and a wonderful 15th century screen as well as other treasures.

Long low thatched Chequers Inn is hidden just outside the village and retains some of its original 16th century exposed beams. Manor courts were held here from at least 1724. A pleasant extension provides bed and breakfast accommodation with one room suitable for disabled use. Food, wine and beer are taken very seriously here. The Chequers offers excellent food with a large menu of à la carte classic dishes as well as varying specials, with an accent on fish. Light bites include ploughman's and jacket potatoes, and there are appetising vegetarian options including Provençal nut Wellington. Dishes such as roasted duck with apricot, pork and peach stuffing are guaranteed to get the gastric juices flowing. The pub offers an ever changing selection of real ales, including Adnam's, Woodforde's Wherry, Fuller's London Pride, Greene King IPA, Elgood's Old Smoothie and local beers from Wolf of Attleborough. As well as a selection of lagers, Strongbow cider is on draught.

The pub is open from Monday to Saturday from 11.30 am to 2.30 pm and 6.30 pm to 11 pm (food served from 12 noon to 2 pm and from 6.30 pm to 9 pm) Sundays 12 noon to 3 pm and 7 pm to 10.30 pm (food from 12 noon to 2 pm and from 7 pm to 9 pm). Telephone: 01953 483360.

- **HOW TO GET THERE:** The Chequers inn is 3 miles south of Watton. Turn right off the A1075 opposite the sign to Griston. The pub is on this road on the right a little way before a crossroads in the centre of Thompson.
- **PARKING:** The Chequers has a large car park, or there is parking behind the church.
- **LENGTH OF THE WALK:** 6 miles (one short cut). Map: OS Explorer 229 Thetford Forest in the Brecks or Explorer 237 Norwich (GR 922969).

THE WALK

1. Turn right out of the pub drive and walk towards a crossroads in Thompson. Turn left at the crossroads and passing a couple of cottages on the left, continue along this leafy lane to another junction by a school. Ignore the lane to the right here and continue on following Church Road as it bears left, passing through fields, towards 14th-century St Martin's collegiate church.

2. Leaving the main road continue on ahead past the church, up a small lane which turns into a broad green track past housing on the right. This meets a cross track (Drove Lane). Turn right and go along this to meet a

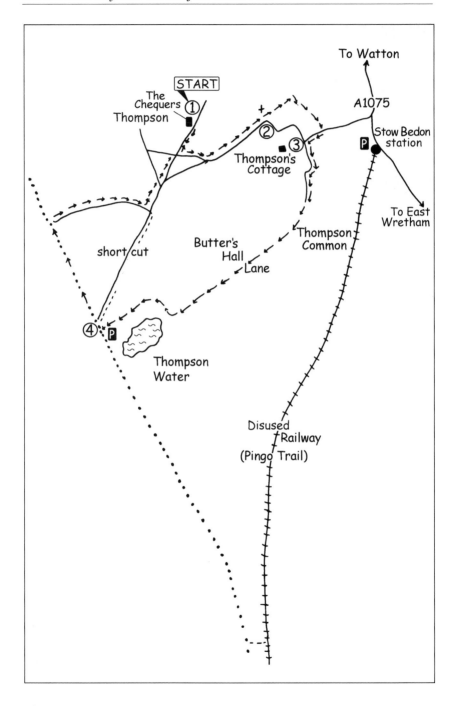

Attractive cottages at Thompson

small lane at a T-junction. Turn right here to another junction at a large grassy triangle.

3. Turn left along a small lane (Butter's Hall Lane). Soon an opening in the trees on the left shows where the Pingo Trail (arrow marked) returns through woodland to its car park. This walk continues down the tree-hung lane on the route of the Pingo Trail.

The road bears to the right over a little bridge and then veers to the left (arrow marker on post). Pass a cottage on the right. The road curves round a bungalow on the right and another dwelling on the left. Pass a bridleway sign into a field on the right. Continue on down the lane winding gently past scattered cottages and stables. Continue on straight ahead along what is now a grassy track (arrow marker), muddy in places, which goes alongside the Thompson reserve on the left and fields on the right. The track narrows near a series of gates on the left. Continue along this tree-hung path. Come into a more open area with a field on the right. Go over an arrow-marked stile back onto the reserve (reserve sign on the right). Pass another arrow marker and go over the middle of an open common area (track marked by the odd post) towards a stile in a fence. Go over the stile and on along another grassy

Near the Pingo Trail

path. Go left over a little bridge, then bear right (signpost on the left) along a path following the edge of a stream through woods. At a broad cross track (arrow marker) turn to the right, cross a bridge of railway sleepers and go along a broad track. After a short distance, turn left along another grassy path (arrow markers) which meanders through varied woodland. At a junction of paths ignore the path ahead and turn left (arrow marker) along a small path through trees with pingo ponds and depressions on either side. At another small cross track (arrow marker) turn right to reach wooden railings. Turn left to look at the huge expanse of Thompson Water. Otherwise keep on ahead to come out onto the Peddars Way (not signposted here).

4. Turn right along this broad track through woodland with the training ground fenced off on the left, marked by No Entry and gun fire warning signs. (Don't worry, you're quite safe.) Cross over a small road (short cut back to Thompson) leading into the training ground, passing lumps of concrete (Long Distance Path marker on left). Continue on ahead where the track becomes more grassy through woodland and then a more open area. The track becomes flinty underfoot and goes into woodland again. Come out between concrete bollards onto another small road leading to the training ground.

Turn right up this leaving the Peddars Way to walk alongside a wood, then farmland. Follow the road to the left where a wide track goes off to the right and come to the outlying houses of Thompson. At a road junction at a grassy triangle, bear right passing housing. Soon at another junction go ahead, ignoring the road bearing off to the right, passing the village hall to reach the crossroads in the centre of the village. Continue on ahead over the crossroads to return to the pub.

 THE PEDDARS WAY - Thompson to Little Cressingham (4½ miles)

When the walk turns right to Thompson carry on along the Peddars Way, continuing on over another road which turns right to Merton and carry on skirting round the edge of woodland on the Merton estate. Bear rightish again, leaving the straight original course of the Way to go along farm tracks passing Home Farm on the right. The route then does a sharp turn to the left and then the right to meet a road from Watton to Bodney. Turn left along the road here to Little Cressingham.

GREAT AND LITTLE CRESSINGHAM
The Windmill
❧

This walk is along lanes (possible with a wheelchair or pushchair) through gentle farmland, with wide views towards woodland on the edge of Breckland. Two lovely churches and an interesting mill punctuate the walk through the valley of the River Wissey.

Great and Little Cressingham are attractive small villages on the edge of Breckland bounded on one side by the Stanford Army Training Ground, a no go area for people but an excellent habitat for wildlife. In Little Cressingham stands St Andrew's church with the ruins of the tower and two bays of the nave probably destroyed in a great storm in the 18th century. Round the corner is a photogenic collection of buildings made up of the unique wind cum water mill in the centre with the stream running by and the gothic pumphouse and miller's house nearby. Great Cressingham has had distinguished ecclesiastical links in the past and its splendid 13th century church of St Michael reflects this with its great buttressed tower and soaring nave, and its hammerbeam roof decorated with carvings of priests instead of the usual angels. Nearby is splendid 16th century Great Cressingham priory.

The Windmill pub lies off the beaten track near the village of Great Cressingham, a few miles south of Swaffham. Its success is due to the family who have been running it for decades. It has been an ale house for a great many years and in former times the Old Bar at the end of the building was the tap room and the landlady would go down into the cellar for a jug of beer to pour out for her regulars. Only a stump is left of the old corn mill nearby which gave the pub its name. Two attractive conservatories lead into a pleasant garden with a play area, there is a games room with pool and darts and private rooms are available for meetings and parties. The menu offers a comprehensive selection of starters, main courses and puddings, or sandwiches and snacks if preferred. Children have a special menu and several of the rooms are suitable for them. On Sundays, there are roasts. The complete menu changes every season and there is a specials board which is changed every Friday. A wide selection of well-kept beers is on offer ranging through Adnam's bitter and Broadside, Greene King IPA, Windy Miller and guest beers. Strongbow and Scrumpy Jack cider are on draught. Lagers are Foster's, Carling, Grolsch, Kronenbourg and Carlsberg. Dogs are welcome if well behaved.

Opening times are from 11 am to 3 pm and from 6 pm to 11 pm. Sunday hours are from 12 noon to 3 pm and from 6 pm to 10.30 pm. Food can be ordered from 12 noon to 2 pm and from 6.30 pm to 10.30 pm. Saturday evening food starts half an hour earlier and Sunday is from 6 pm to 10 pm. Telephone: 01760 756232.

- **HOW TO GET THERE:** To reach Great Cressingham, turn off the A1065 about halfway between Swaffham and Mundford. The pub is near the river Wissey, just before turning into the village.
- **PARKING:** The pub has plenty of parking.
- **Length of the walk:** 5½ miles (with one short cut). Map: OS Explorer 236 King's Lynn, Downham Market and Swaffham (GR 854019).

THE WALK

1. Turn left out of the pub and walk along the road crossing the River Wissey. Continue along the road ignoring the left turn to Great Cressingham.

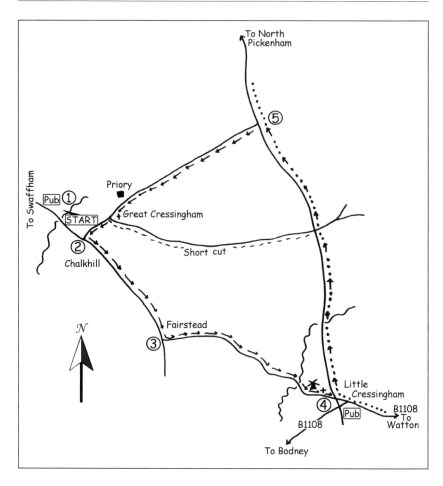

2. Pass an old Methodist chapel and go uphill to some more houses at Chalkhill. Continue for some distance along the road which now passes near the training area. Ignore a green lane on the left and follow the road as it curves right to a road junction by a cottage.

3. Turn left down Fairstead Lane (again signposted to Little Cressingham). The lane wiggles on for some distance with views of the windmill and St Andrew's church with its ruined west end. Eventually the road goes over a little red brick bridge over a tributary of the river Wissey, with the picturesque combination of the windmill and the miller's house on the left. The mill's power source is wind and water combined and is unique. It is open May to October on the second

The windmill at Little Cressingham is open to the public

Sunday in the month from 2 pm to 5 pm. The lane continues winding past the half-ruined church, some houses, then reaches a crossroads in Little Cressingham.

4. Turn left here and go ahead along the Peddars Way (wooden signpost on the right). Pass the Old Rectory on the left and, leaving the houses of the village, wend your way down this lane through fields edged with trees. Cross a white bridge over a stream and continue following the gentle curves of the lane up a gentle slope. There are lovely wide views over open farmland towards woods. The lane bends to the left and comes to a crossroads (go left for a short cut). Go straight over (wooden signpost on the right). Continue on along the lane which is decked with a wide variety of wild flowers in summer.

5. After a long gentle bend to the left, turn left off the route of the Peddars Way down a lane which bears a sign 'No Entry for Military Vehicles'. This is Priory Road leading into Great Cressingham. Pass an interesting complex of derelict buildings on the right. There is now a good view of Great Cressingham church on the hill ahead. A splendid

The Gothic pump house at Little Cressingham mill

16th-century priory (private) lies nearby on the right. The road bends gently and enters the 30 mph limit to pass village houses and the church with its fine 15th-century tower on the left. At a road junction turn right, signposted to Little Cressingham. There is a splendid village sign at the junction. Pass some flint houses and cottages and a pretty old school among more modern buildings and at the next junction turn right back to the Windmill pub.

 THE PEDDARS WAY – Priory Road, Great Cressingham to South Pickenham Crossroads (1¼ miles)

To continue along the Peddars Way, carry on along the lane when the circular walk turns left, passing Caudle Common on the left and crossing a tributary of the River Wissey. At a crossroads near South Pickenham just past Hall Farm on the right, continue on ahead along a small lane which is the route of the Peddars Way and part of the next circular walk.

NORTH PICKENHAM AND HOUGHTON COMMON
The Blue Lion
❧❀❧

Here, in the depths of the Norfolk countryside, Peddars Way provided a route for pilgrims passing through to Walsingham via Castle Acre. Starting from a pub used for centuries by travellers, the walk goes through farmland to Houghton Common near the picturesque ivy clad ruins of St Mary's, Houghton on the Hill. It then drops into the valley of the little River Wissey near South Pickenham to return through the water meadows of Houghton Carr and Houghton Springs to reach North Pickenham where there was once a chapel and a hermitage.

The Pickenhams lie on the centuries old pilgrim's route to Walsingham taken by even the highest in the land. Records show that Henry VIII's first queen, Catherine of Aragon, came this way and there are many religious sites in the vicinity including a chapel, hermitage and St Paul's holy well outside North Pickenham. Maybe a hostelry such as the 500 year old Blue Lion in North Pickenham sheltered the pilgrims and gave them sustenance.

Today the Grade 2 listed Blue Lion, a freehouse, is a pleasant local pub with plenty and varied entertainment. The welcoming atmosphere is enhanced by a cheery fire in winter; in the games room, where children are welcome, is a collection of World War 2 memorabilia connected with the nearby war time American base. Food ranges from sandwiches, jackets and ploughman's to typical pub dishes such as ham and eggs or beef and onion pie. On Sundays there is a choice of traditional roasts. The pub offers several real ales including Abbot, Greene King IPA and Speckled Hen with guest beers, such as Elgood's Mad Dog, changing with the season. There is a choice of draught lagers, Scrumpy Jack cider is on draught, and there is always coffee on tap. Dogs are allowed in the garden. The pub is open all day every day from 11 am to 11.30 pm (Sunday 12 noon to 10.30 pm) and food can usually be ordered from about 12 noon to 2 pm and from 7 pm to 9 pm. Telephone: 01760 440289

- **HOW TO GET THERE**: North Pickenham is signposted from the B1077 which runs from Swaffham to Watton.
- **PARKING:** In the pub car park or carefully in the village.
- **LENGTH OF THE WALK:** 5½ miles (two short cuts possible). Map: OS Explorer 236 King's Lynn, Downham Market and Swaffham (GR 864069)

THE WALK

1. Turn left out of the Blue Lion pub and walk left along Houghton Lane.

2. At the next T-junction turn right (signposted to South Pickenham) for about a quarter of a mile and then on a slight bend turn left up a mysterious overgrown track closely hedged on either side. This carries on for some distance. Eventually the track bursts out onto a wide area of grass edging a field. Carry on along the hedgerow on the right. A track leading to St Mary's church, Houghton, and the short cut, goes off to the right. The walk continues on alongside the hedge, past some conifers masking new tree planting behind. Ignore another (private) green lane coming in from the right and continue on round the field bearing to the left. The track then bends to the right again

35

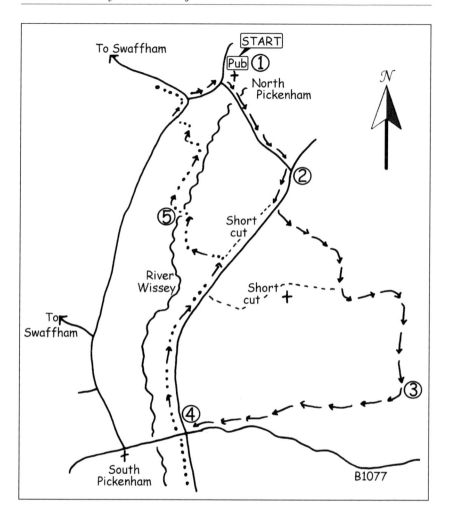

and continues more or less straight on with poplars on the right. The poplars end and soon after, the green track bears to the right and there are buildings over the field on the left. The track bends left, then immediately right and comes out at a lane by a public footpath signpost. A farm drive goes to left and right, the walk goes ahead down the small lane between fields.

3. Turn right at the concrete pad, and follow the hard farm track through fields towards woods ahead. The hard track swings right. Continue ahead at a wooden signpost into a field. At the end of the field

The church of St Andrew, North Pickering

there is a little bridge over a ditch leading into the next field. The path should carry on straight through the field but was not cleared through the crop when I walked, and if you find this to be so, turn left and right to skirt round the field to a gap leading onto the road. Turn right along the road and walk to a crossroads.

4. For the main walk join the Peddars Way (wooden signpost on left) by turning right at the crossroads along a small lane passing a derelict red brick cottage on the right. Ignore all the farm sidetracks until just before a right-hand bend in the road where a wooden Peddars Way signpost on the left indicates that the path now travels inside the hedge. Carry on walking along this path with the hedge and lane on the right. Cross over a driveway leading towards Houghton Springs. (The short cut passing derelict St Mary's church rejoins the route from the right.) Carry on along the field edge to a signpost at the end of the field. Turn left along the edge of the field with a hedge on the right. At the end of the field an arrow marker points to the right along the edge of another field. Just before a knot of trees, a wooden signpost points left up steps and over a stile into a field. The path then skirts along the left-hand edge of this little meadow and goes over a wooden bridge over the river.

5. Continue ahead along the edge of another small meadow. At the corner is a plastic arrow marker. Turn right bordering the edge of the meadow, with a ditch on the left. At the end of the meadow cross a stile, go up steps and turn right along the edge of another field. Go through a gap in the hedge into the next field and bear left (arrow marker). Bear right at the corner of the field alongside the fence and hedge of a school on the left, then go right to meet the road. Turn right up the road to a junction with a Peddars Way signpost.

The Peddars Way goes left, initially along the Swaffham road. Our walk turns right and goes through the village of North Pickenham passing the village sign and ignoring all turn offs to reach another road junction and the Blue Lion pub.

 THE PEDDARS WAY – North Pickenham to Castle Acre (7¼ miles)

From North Pickenham, the Peddars Way passes first of all along the Swaffham road, carrying on to a green lane at a T-junction. The Way is now known as Procession Lane either because of the many groups of pilgrims making their way to Walsingham, or possibly recalling the ceremony of 'beating the bounds' as several parish boundaries meet here as well as several important tracks and roads. The route then carries on over the A47 and onto a metalled lane which swings left to join the Sporle road, turning a short distance to the right along this, before going left again onto a green lane passing Palgrave Hall on the left. At a T-junction with a small metalled road, the Peddars Way bears left along the road near the sites of the two deserted villages of Little and Great Palgrave to reach Bartholomew's Hills where several roads and tracks converge. Cross the A1065 taking the road signposted to South Acre, reaching another crossroads. Go on ahead along a small lane which bears right to the ford below Castle Acre.

NEWTON BY CASTLE ACRE
The George and Dragon
❧

This area of Norfolk takes you right back in time. You could be a pilgrim travelling down the lanes on a journey to the shrine at Walsingham just as people have travelled for hundreds of years. The route goes through the water meadows of the River Nar to travel one of the prettiest parts of the Peddars Way, from a ford near the priory ruins, then through lanes to an ancient bailey gate with a Norman castle mound nearby. The walk returns to Newton through a beautiful area of common land to reach Newton Mill on the Nar Valley Way.

Medieval Castle Acre is one of the most exciting villages in Norfolk. Pretty little lanes run uphill from the River Nar to approach the Norman castle via the beautiful 13th century bailey gate, or cross the ford to go to the ruins of the Cluniac priory founded in 1090 and thought to be the best monastic ruins in East Anglia. At the centre of the village is a tree-lined green surrounded by pretty cottages (some of which date back to the 15th century), shops, two pubs and two tea rooms. The 15th century church of St James the Great, with its fine font cover and screen, stands a little further on.

The small settlement of Newton, just outside Castle Acre, is not much more than a manor house and the George and Dragon pub, but it boasts a most interesting little Saxon church with a central tower. The pub is on the busy main road, but inside the atmosphere is traditional and peaceful – no machines, no pub games, just good traditional pub food in pleasant surroundings with a cheery open fire in winter. The building dates back to 1750, and stands in two and a half acres of land which can accommodate tents and touring caravans. The beer garden with a children's play area enjoys extensive views over Castle Acre.

The George and Dragon is a freehouse and keeps excellent real ales including Adnam's, Greene King IPA, Coors and often Woodforde's Wherry among the changing guest beers. Also on draught are Carling and Grolsch lagers, Guinness and local Aspall cider. The food is traditional pub fare reasonably priced with special offers for pensioners and a two for one steak night. There are snacks such as jacket potatoes, hot baguettes and a farmer's lunch (a ploughman's which includes soup) as well as more substantial dishes. Specials are written up on the board and there is a Sunday roast. Opening hours are from 12 noon to 3 pm and from 6 pm to 11 pm (10.30 pm on Sunday). Food is available from 12 noon to 2.30 pm and from 6.30 pm to 9 pm (later Friday and Saturday). Telephone: 01760 755046.

- **How to get there:** The George and Dragon at Newton is on the A1065 Swaffham to Fakenham road about 10 miles north of Swaffham.
- **Parking:** There is a large car park at the rear of the pub. There is also parking by Castle Acre green or in the signposted priory car park nearby.
- **Length of the walk:** 5¾ miles (with possible short cuts). Map: OS Explorer 236 King's Lynn, Downham Market and Swaffham (GR 830154). Wear long trousers and long sleeves for this walk as some paths can be overgrown.

The Walk

1. Turn right out of the pub and then go right again up the lane by the pub passing a three storey, red brick house and then cottages on the left and carrying on to where the lane forks. Take the right hand fork and walk on for some distance. There is a huge chalk quarry over the field

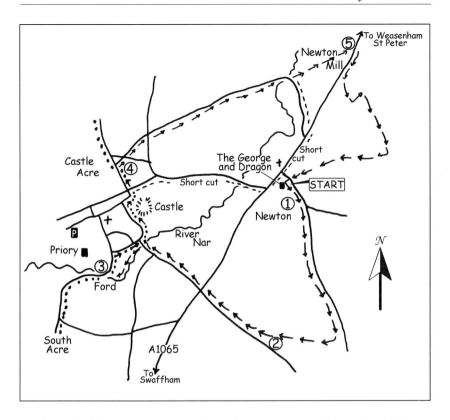

on the left. The lane rises gently and passes a wood on a bend. Soon after this a bridleway from the left meets the road. Turn right opposite this along a field edge following a rather rough and weedy footpath. Pass some large oak trees and then a small copse. Skirt left to the road.

2. Turn right down a pretty lane from which, in gaps between the hedges and trees, there are views over Castle Acre and its church standing high on a hillside. Come to the busy A1065 between Swaffham and Fakenham. Cross carefully and go ahead down another pretty lane opposite (weight restriction) – the view of the castle mound is improving all the time and a little further on there is a good view of the priory ahead. At a junction with a bigger road bear right, cross the bridge over the River Nar, and just before a junction named Blind Lane, go over a stile to the left into the water meadows by the river. Follow an embanked path all along the river (it does two loops turning right back on itself). The reed-fringed river is hung with willows as it nears a lane.

41

The ancient ruins of Castle Acre Priory

Go over a stile and a little wooden bridge and turn left to follow the lane round to the ford and footbridge over the river. There are lovely views of the priory from this point and sections of ancient wall stand by the lane in some places.

3. You are now following the Peddars Way which has come in from South Acre. Turn back up the lane and continue on along it passing the stile crossed earlier from the water meadows. Soon, at the next junction, turn right up a lane (Blind Lane) at a grassy triangle. Continue straight on where another small lane (Chimney Street) goes to the left and come out onto a more main road at a grassy triangle with an arrow marker on a post. Follow the Peddars Way left up Castle Hill passing the Old Red Lion on the right. Cuckstool Lane on the right gives access to the castle if you want to make a detour. Pass two more small lanes going off to the left and carry on ahead through the magnificent bailey gate. Stocks Green is on the left if you need to stop for refreshment. At the further end of the green is the interesting church of St James the Great and even further on is the entrance to the priory. To continue the walk, follow the Peddars Way to the right from the bailey gate along the High Street, then turn left. At a crossroads go straight over. There is a short cut along the road to the right, back to Newton if required. The full walk goes on ahead to another road junction passing cottages on the left and a recreation ground on the right.

4. Here we leave the Peddars Way and take the right turn signposted to Rougham and come to another village green. On the green is another crossroads where we continue on ahead along Archer Lane still signposted to Rougham. Pass a white cottage on the right and continue out into the countryside along this narrow lane. At a further junction at a grassy triangle, leave the road to Rougham which bears left and cross to a lane ahead. A further lane to the right goes back to Castle Acre. The lane ahead meanders down into a valley passing a lovely area of common on the right. Further down on the right a little way into Broadmeadow Common is a hidden pond frequented by ducks and geese. A right of way is signposted to the right passing a house at Fiddler's Green. The route of this walk continues on up the lane passing another house with a track behind. The lane goes through another area of common with the river hidden somewhere on the right.

Bear right near Mill Farm on the left and go over a bridge in front of Newton Mill and cottage. This is now part of the Nar Valley Way, a 34 mile walk running from King's Lynn to the Museum of Rural Life at Gressenhall. (For a short cut, follow the lane bearing right to reach the main road and right again back to the pub.) For the main walk turn left beyond the mill along a broad stony bridleway with a little green on the left going down to the river. Where the stony track swings to the left, carry on ahead through wooden posts passing a cottage on the left with a dovecote in its garden. Carry on along a broad hedged track to go through more wooden barriers at the main road.

5. Cross carefully and, ignoring the lane leading to the Lexhams, turn very sharp right walking along the old road which is inside the hedge alongside the main road. At the end of the field by the roadside there is a signpost at a gateway. Take this broad track to the left which goes alongside a hedge with an open field on the right. It swings left going through a rough common area and then bears right again. The track goes through a gateway with a plastic arrow marker and continues on as a grassy path to the right of a fenced off rough area. Again the way is rather overgrown but obvious. This carries on for quite some distance to meet a hedgerow. Carry on ahead into a field. There was no clear path left when I walked but keep persevering because you soon come

A ford on the Peddars Way at Castle Acre

to the end of the field where a signpost points back and to the right.

Turn right along a now broad grassy track with good views over the valley on the right. Pass farm storage tanks on a concrete pad and carry on along the farm track as it curves round gently. Ignore another track going off to the left at a bend. The track is now broad and stony and the houses and church of Newton are in view with Castle Acre beyond. Pass some dilapidated flint farm buildings on the right and then a three storey, red brick farmhouse. Come out by white gates and turn right and then left to the pub.

 THE PEDDARS WAY – Castle Acre to Harpley Dams (6¼ miles)

The Peddars Way leaves Castle Acre on the Great Massingham Road. Look out for the point where the footpath has been rerouted behind the hedge away from traffic for some distance. Further on where the Massingham Road swings to the right keep on ahead onto a grassy farm track. The Peddars Way now carries straight on for several miles, sometimes grassy sometimes stony, occasionally metalled, through remote countryside. It crosses several roads until it meets the main A148. Just up the lane from here is Harpley Dams where the next walk joins the long distance route.

HARPLEY AND HOUGHTON HALL
The Rose and Crown

*A*ll the elements which make the English countryside especially beautiful are present in this lovely walk. The ancient track of the Peddars Way passes Bronze Age tumuli near the superb woods of the Houghton estate, with historic Houghton Hall. Houghton has its own attractive estate village while the neighbouring village of Harpley contains pretty cottages, and an architecturally magnificent church enfolded by leafy lanes and rolling fields.

The attractive small village of Harpley, just off the A148 King's Lynn to Cromer road, has a hidden secret – its 14th and 15th century church of St Lawrence is a little gem. It has splendid Decorated Gothic workmanship, lovely carvings in wood and stone, and angels holding up the roof. It stands apart from the main part of the village, not far from Harpley Hall with its large lake almost hidden in woodland. The village consists of a huddle of old houses and cottages, with a square of Dutch-gabled almshouses and a decorative brick chapel of 1871. The pub is in the middle on the main village street. The attractive exterior of this 16th century pantiled building is decorated with cheerful hanging baskets. The interior is pleasant and traditional, with two open fires which are lit in winter. Through the open bar is a restaurant area leading to a sheltered and enclosed garden with seating for al fresco eating. A bowl of water is provided for dogs. The pub is closed on Mondays and there is no food on Tuesday lunchtime. The rest of the week opening hours are from 12 noon to 3 pm and from 7 pm to 11 pm (10.30 pm on Sundays). Food is served from 12 noon to 2 pm and 7 pm to 9 pm.

The pub offers Greene King IPA, plus two guest beers, a selection of lagers and a draught cider. Food is home-cooked and of the traditional pub variety, with a changing menu. Children's dishes and vegetarian options are included. Telephone: 01485 520577.

- **How to get there:** Harpley is on the A148 between Hillington and East Rudham. Take the first right signposted to the village, when coming from the Hillington direction. The pub is on the main street in the centre of the village.
- **Parking:** In front of the pub or in the lane by Peddars Way in Harpley Dams.
- **Length of walk:** 7½ miles (with several opportunities for short cuts). Map: OS Explorer 250 Norfolk Coast West (GR 789258).

The Walk

1. Leave the pub and turn left down the main street of the village of Harpley for a short distance. Turn right down Brickyard Lane (signpost) passing Rose Cottage on the right. The lane becomes a grassy path between hedges. Follow it through a small copse and then along the edge of a field by a hedge, eventually emerging onto a lane. Bear left along this (signpost) ignoring a bridleway which goes off on the left. There is now an open field on the left (signpost). Continue on through gates to the road. Cross carefully and walk to the left for a short distance, then bear right, off the main road down a small lane. At a road junction by cottages (Harpley Dams) go straight ahead onto the Peddars Way (there is an acorn signpost on the right), ignoring the other lane on the right unless using it for a short cut.

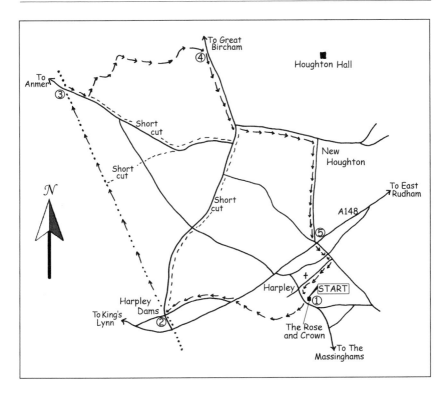

● **2.** The Peddars Way here is a broad green lane with stretches of
hedges and mature trees passing through rolling farmland. Knots
of trees and depressions in the fields along the route of the Way in this
area are probably 18th-century pits from which marl was dug to use as
fertiliser. After about a mile Crow Hall comes into view over on the left
and the hedgerow on the right ends. Here a bridleway turns off the
Peddars Way to the right. This can be used as a short cut via fields but
misses out a lovely walk through the woods of the Houghton estate. For
the short cut continue on this track with a hedge on the right, veering
round a newly planted copse to meet a small lane. Go left for a few steps
then cross the lane and turn right alongside a hedge (signpost). Follow
the path as it curves round a pit at a corner planted with trees and
continue bearing slightly right to meet the Anmer to Harpley road at a
corner near woods. Ignore a broad track to the immediate right and
carry on rightish along the lane following it as it bends to the right. At a
T-junction turn left and go on a little way to a junction of roads at a large
grassy triangle (Old Bottom) where the longer walk comes in. For the

47

The almshouses in Harpley

longer walk, continue on along the Peddars Way for another mile. There are the mounds of tumuli in the fields on the right in the area known as Harpley Common.

3. Just past a large mound quite near to the track turn sharp right (there is a Peddars Way signpost over the road) and walk along the Anmer road bordering the woods of the Houghton estate. For a short cut continue on down the road. For the main walk, after a short distance, go left along a signposted track through a white painted gate into the woods. Go ahead up a broad ride which soon goes over a cross path. Carry on further and go over another cross path. At the next junction of paths turn off the track which goes on ahead and then bears left, and bear right along a path through woods edged with dark fir trees eventually bearing slightly round to the left. Coming to a T-junction on a bend, ignore the right branch and go left, soon leaving the trees and crossing over an open green space towards a cottage. Just before the cottage there is a track through the grass. Turn right along this and walk alongside woods towards a barn at the bottom of the open green area. Near the barn turn left along a gravelled drive which bears right through trees to white gates leading onto a road (signpost).

4. Over the road is a pretty lodge restored by the Landmark Trust. Turn right and walk along the small road through lovely woodland for just over half a mile. At a road junction near a large grassy triangle (Old Bottom) bear left (signposted Houghton ¾ mile). The continuation of the road goes to Harpley Dams and is where the short cuts come in.

Walk along the wide road bordered by woods on the left past imposing Home Farm and a stately avenue of trees giving a view of Palladian Houghton Hall (built in the 1720s for Sir Robert Walpole – Britain's first Prime Minister). Turn right by the Hall gates and walk up through the estate village of New Houghton. The road with its wide verges continues through an avenue of mature limes before narrowing as it reaches the main A148 road near a small lane on the right.

5. Cross the road carefully and go down the lane opposite into Harpley, passing lovely Manor Farm on the left. Go straight on at a crossroads and continue down Back Street. After a short distance turn right up Church Street, with a view of an old mill over the fields. Pass a trig point on the left and ignore footpaths signposted to right and left. Pass the lovely church of St Lawrence. At a road junction go left passing an interesting

The Victorian chapel, Harpley

courtyard of old almshouses. Pass the village shop, and then the old Methodist church to return to the pub.

 THE PEDDARS WAY – Harpley Common to Great Bircham (1½ miles)

From Harpley Common, the Peddars Way continues as a broad green lane passing over the Anmer to Houghton road near Bronze Age tumuli and the B1153 Flitcham to Great Bircham road near Anmer Minque to go on to a junction of tracks near Great Bircham.

GREAT BIRCHAM AND FOX COVERT
The King's Head

Abundant wild flowers and wildlife, especially hares, can be seen on this walk along broad green lanes through open farmland. The lanes were probably old drove roads linking the Peddars Way to the three Bircham settlements. The views are dominated by Great Bircham windmill, complete with sails, which the walk passes as it returns to the village. This is well worth visiting and provides a welcome opportunity for a cup of tea during the summer months.

The three Birchams – Great Bircham, Bircham Newton and Bircham Tofts – each had its own church, though St Andrew's at Toft is now a ruin. All three communities are associated with the nearby Houghton estate. The area of Bircham Common and Heath to the south is the site of four barrows which contained Bronze Age funerary urns. St Mary's church at Great Bircham dates back to the 15th century but has a lovely 13th century doorway and some Norman work. In the churchyard is a Second World War monument which remembers the RAF station at Bircham Newton. Tiny 13th century All Saints' church at Bircham Newton is charming. The old pews still have candle holders, an unusual stone coffin lid is carved with the figure of a Roman Catholic priest, and on the south wall is a monument to Nelson's grandson. Just outside Great Bircham stands a fine windmill built around 1846 which has been restored to working order and is well worth a visit.

The King's Head hotel at Great Bircham on the edge of the Royal Sandringham estate, is a fine old building originally built at the instigation of Queen Victoria. The hotel has recently been renovated and the bars now offer a modern relaxed style of hospitality with open fires and a convivial atmosphere. The restaurant has a menu based on the great classic dishes using quality food cooked simply with fresh local ingredients, and all reasonably priced. Coffee, tea and snacks are available all day. The local beers include Greene King and Adnam's with a selection of designer beers and lager plus Guinness on draught.

The hotel has five en suite bedrooms at the moment. The King's Head stands in large grounds offering plenty of parking and al fresco eating and drinking in attractive courtyard gardens. Well behaved dogs and children are welcome. Licensing hours are from 11 am to 11 pm from Monday to Saturday and 12 noon to 10.30 pm on Sunday. Meals are served at reasonable times within those hours. Telephone: 01485 578265.

- **HOW TO GET THERE:** Great Bircham is on the B1153 between Docking and Flitcham. The hotel is on the main road opposite a turning to Houghton.
- **PARKING:** There is a large car park to the rear of the hotel or in the village street.
- **LENGTH OF THE WALK:** 4¾ miles (with one option for a short cut). Map: Explorer 250 Norfolk Coast West (GR 766322).

THE WALK

1. Turn right out of the pub and walk along the road a little way to a small grassy triangle where a broad track goes off to the right between old farm buildings and cottages. Keep on along this broad old drove road which stretches straight out ahead for about 1½ miles. Ignore any tracks off. Some parts are designated as wildlife areas. It is easy to imagine driving flocks of sheep or geese to market down these old lanes. Most of the route is hedged on either side for shelter.

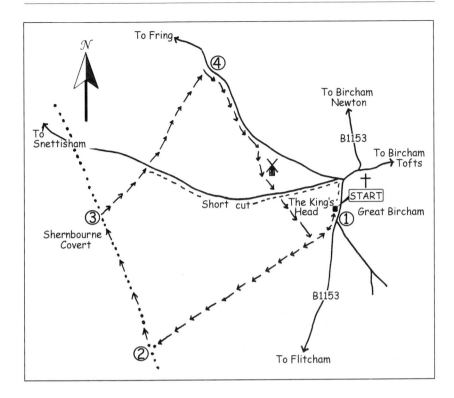

2. Eventually the track comes to a point where several tracks meet. The Peddars Way runs at right angles to this first track and is signposted on the left here. Turn right along the Peddars Way which is similar in size and feel to the first track and indeed must often have been used as a drove road itself. This track is more undulating and there are still views over to the windmill on the right. Again there is a large wildlife conservation area. To the left there are various wooded coverts. Keep on along the Peddars Way for just over a mile passing Shernbourne covert over the field on the left.

3. Just opposite the end of this, leave the Peddars Way and turn right along yet another broad green drove road. This one is not quite so straight and the hedgerows are studded with fine old oak trees. After some distance the track crosses the small road which leads from Snettisham to Great Bircham (which could be used as a short cut) and continues on. The land here becomes undulating and there is evidence of old pit workings on either side. On the right a stark line of conifers

The working mill at Great Bircham also has a tea room

delineates the skyline (Fox Covert) and on the left is a copse of mixed woodland and scrub. Here the windmill is hidden from view. Keep following the gentle curves and undulations of this lane until it comes out onto a tiny lane between a pump building and a strip of woodland (old osier carr – a fenny copse of willow).

4. This pretty lane leads from Fring to Great Bircham. Turn right along it with the windmill now in view. Continue on for over half a mile until a small lane leads off to the right to pass the windmill which makes an attractive group with the miller's cottage to one side, and all the associated barns. The mill looks much as it did when it was built in 1846 (earlier mills stood on the same site). It is in working order and visitors can climb up five storeys to look at the view or see a video of milling on the ground floor. There is a small bakery attached to the mill building where food is baked in a 200 year old coal-fired peel oven. The tearooms offer home-made refreshments, and gifts connected with milling and baking. In the old stables are ponies for pony rides, or cycles for hire.

Continue on from the mill and cross the Snettisham to Bircham road. The track becomes a broad green ride at the edge of an open field on the right and another area of wildlife conservation. This green ride meets the green lane taken on the outward journey. Turn left up it and turn left again at the grassy triangle to go back to the pub.

 THE PEDDARS WAY - Great Bircham to Fring Road, Sedgeford (2¼ miles)

From the countryside near Great Bircham dominated by the windmill, the Way continues as a broad green lane crossing two small roads on the outskirts of Fring to reach a third road leading to Sedgeford at Fring Cross (once the site of a wayside cross).

SEDGEFORD, FRING CROSS AND LITTLEPORT

The King William IV

This pleasant walk begins at Sedgeford, on the slope of a pretty valley through which the little River Heacham runs. Near here an amazing Iron Age torc was found (now in the British Museum). The walk skirts the grounds of Sedgeford Hall and continues on through farmland to a curious building known as the Magazine House, once used as an ammunition store during the Civil War.

Sedgeford is a mysterious village clinging to the side of a valley at the bottom of which trickles the little Heacham river passing an ancient spring called Lady Well. The 13th century church of St Mary, with its 11th century round tower, lies down the slope near the remnant of the medieval village green. The Hall on the Fring road is Queen Anne. Just outside the village in the hamlet of Littleport is the Magazine House used by Sir Hamon L'Estrange as a store for ammunition in his resistance to the Parliamentarians in the Civil War. The Sedgeford torc, dating from the Iron Age and now in the British Museum, was found in the 1960s. In recent years, archaeological digs in Sedgeford have unearthed a wealth of finds which explain the village's past importance.

The village pub, the King William IV, is an excellent place for warming and sustaining refreshment after a dig or a walk. It combines a popular local with a sought after eating-place for people from miles around, who know that they will get a good meal with generous quantities. The building was a farm until it became a pub in 1836, since when it has gradually increased in size.

Meals can be taken in the bar, or there are two restaurant areas, and a pleasant conservatory with tables outside for summer eating overlooking the tree-lined valley below. There are smoking and non-smoking areas and children are welcome. The menu combines old favourites such as gammon steak and pie of the day with more unusual dishes such as red onion and stilton tartlet as a starter and wild mushroom crepes in a port wine sauce as a main dish. For pudding the apricot and brandy bread and butter pudding sounds delicious. The pub is a freehouse and serves excellent real ales, usually Greene King and Adnam's plus mid-range guest beers each week. Opening hours are: 11 am to 3 pm and 6.30 pm to 11 pm (10.30 pm Sundays). Food is served from 12 noon to 2 pm and from 7 pm to 9 pm. There is no food on Mondays. Telephone: 01485 571765.

- **How to get there:** The King William IV is in the centre of Sedgeford on the B1454, midway between Heacham and Docking, not far from Hunstanton.
- **Parking:** To the side and rear of the pub.
- **Length of the walk:** 3¼ miles. Map: OS Explorer 250 Norfolk Coast West (GR 710365).

The Walk

1. Turn right out of the pub and walk along the Docking road passing a left turn which leads to Ringstead. Pass some terraces of pretty cottages on the left and come to a small triangular green with a war memorial on it. Where the main road bends to the left, turn right towards Fring along a lovely lane bordered by a low carr stone wall beyond which a meadow slopes down towards trees and the river. On the left is a high tree-covered bank. Pass some pretty cottages and the lovely woods and

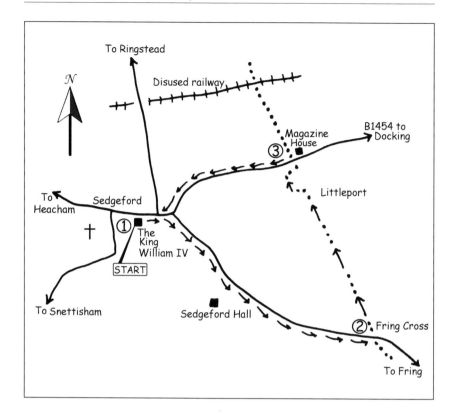

grounds of Sedgeford Hall on the right. Beyond the pleasant old buildings of Glover's Farm, the lane continues to wind through open countryside with plenty of trees. Continue on to where the Peddars Way (signposted) crosses the lane at Fring Cross just before a small bridge. This is the site of an old wayside cross and once there was a ford over the Heacham river here.

2. Walk to the left up a broad green verge at the edge of a field along a sweeping hedgerow with a newly planted copse on the right. Look back over a lovely vista of fields broken up by hedges and copses. Continue on, passing Dovehill Wood on the left. Shortly after this an arrow marker on a post points the way through the hedgerow after which it continues on again, this time with the hedgerow on the right. At the corner of the field carry on through a hedgerow (with an arrow marker) and turn left for a short distance then right again (arrowed) to go along a narrow fenced path eventually passing a row of

The Magazine House was built around 1640

cottages in the hamlet of Littleport. There are views to your right over Docking church and the parkland of Docking Hall.

3. Cross the Sedgeford to Docking road and make a short detour to the right to see the Magazine House, probably built in about 1640 by Sir Hamon Le Strange to store powder and weapons and later used by the Royalist cause in the Civil War. The Peddars Way goes down the drive past this unusual building, but to continue the walk, turn back down the road walking along the pavement on the right-hand side from the hamlet of Fairstead through fields to the outlying houses of Sedgeford, which are an interesting mix of local carr stone, white clunch and pantiles. Pass a pretty, brick Methodist chapel on the right and continue on over a side road leading to a modern estate. After this the pavement goes along the old carr stone wall of a farm. At the little green where the Fring road goes off, bear right and retrace your steps back to the pub.

If you have time, continue on past the pub turning left to visit the 13th-century church with its round Saxon tower with a later octagonal cap. Beyond the church a path leads down steps to the pretty Heacham river.

The 13th century church of St Mary, Sedgeford

 THE PEDDARS WAY - Docking Road, Sedgeford to Ringstead (2½ miles)

The route of the Peddars Way carries on from the Docking Road, crossing a dismantled railway, to run in a pretty straight line (apart from a dogleg to left and right at a track which leads right to Courtyard Farm camping barn), passing through open farmland as a green lane to the village of Ringstead.

OLD HUNSTANTON, RINGSTEAD AND HOLME BEACH

The Ancient Mariner

An interesting and varied walk through two pretty villages built from beautiful local stone. The route leaves Old Hunstanton and its lovely church, which has links with former smuggling activity, to reach Ringstead via green lanes backed by the woods of Old Hunstanton Hall and Ringstead Downs Nature Reserve. The walk then goes downhill through fields and lanes, with good sea views towards the beach at Holme-next-the-Sea.

Until mid-Victorian times when the railway came to Hunstanton, Old Hunstanton was a small huddle of old fishermen's cottages between the late 15th century Hall and the sea. There are still pretty lanes of old cottages amidst more modern development. The church of St Mary the Virgin dating back to the early 1300s was built by members of the Le Strange family whose monuments are a feature of the interior. It stands in a picturesque spot near the gates of the Hall and the village duck pond. The churchyard is famous for two 18th century memorials to revenue men murdered by local smugglers. The Le Strange family developed the land on the cliff into the seaside resort of Hunstanton using the distinctive local carr stone.

The nearby village of Ringstead up on the hill used to have three parish churches – the only remaining one being 14th century St Andrew's. The ruins of St Andrew's chapel at Ringstead Parva can be seen at the end of Ringstead Downs. Ringstead also has an excellent pub, the Gin Trap, passed on this walk.

Even though it is officially part of the Le Strange Arms hotel, its old beams, open fires, tiled floors and interesting nautical artefacts give the Ancient Mariner its own identity and the feel of a traditional pub. Children are not allowed in the main bar but there are two family rooms – one up an open staircase. Dogs are allowed in the tiled bar area only. The non smoking downstairs family room, again with a sea view, leads on to a garden and the hotel lawn where there is a play area and access to the beach. This popular pub is open all day in summer from the May Bank Holiday until at least the end of September. At other times its hours are from 11 am to 3 pm and from 6 pm to 11 pm (open all day on Friday, Saturday and Sunday). Sunday winter hours are 12 noon to 10.30 pm. Bar meals are served in winter from 12 noon to 2.30 pm and from 6.30 pm to 9 pm while restaurant hours are 12 noon to 2 pm and 7 pm to 9 pm. Meals are served all day in summer.

The menu is the same whether you choose to eat in the bars or the restaurant. There is a good choice of standard pub food at reasonable prices. Seafood is a feature and, as the pub is popular with families, there is a special children's menu. There are interesting dishes on the specials board such as salmon and dill fishcakes, and hot apple and blueberry pie with custard.

The three permanent real ales are Adnam's bitter and Broadside, and Bass. There are changing guest ales depending on the season. Lagers are Stella Artois and Grolsch. The two draught ciders are Scrumpy Jack and Olde English. Wines are available. Telephone: 01485 534411.

- **HOW TO GET THERE:** The pub is just off the A149 coast road as it bends sharply to the right on leaving Hunstanton and entering Old Hunstanton. Look for a lane on the left signposted to the Le Strange Arms and a craft and antiques gallery. The Ancient Mariner is not far down here on the left.
- **PARKING:** There is limited parking opposite the pub, but plenty at the hotel. There is a car park near the beach at Holme-next-the-Sea or at Ringstead Downs.

- **LENGTH OF THE WALK:** 7¼ miles (with two short cuts). Map: OS Explorer 250 Norfolk Coast West (GR 681424).

THE WALK

1. From the pub turn left for a few paces to a small crossroads then turn right here up Sea Lane. Continue on over a crossroads (a private road goes to the left) and come out onto the main A149 road opposite Lodge Hotel. Turn left and walk along a narrow pavement. Cross over Hamilton Road and continue on to the Neptune pub on the left. Beyond this is Caley Hall Motel on a slightly staggered crossroads.

2. Turn right up the lane (with a cottage on the corner) leading to Old Hunstanton church. This walk turns right at the next road junction but it is worth taking a small detour straight on to look at the church in its beautiful setting.

For the walk go back to the road junction, turn left and continue on along a lane passing a modern house, then through woodland passing the drive into Cliff Farm. Where the lane bends rightish, turn left down a broad grassy track (with a bench on the junction) hedged on both sides. This green lane curves on for quite some distance then, near the cluster of buildings of Lodge Farm, it turns sharp left then right, passing a carr stone wall bisecting a meadow, to come out onto another stony track. Turn left along this. Soon there is a grassy triangle with a lodge guarding a drive to Hunstanton Hall tucked away on the left. Turn sharp right here and continue on for another three quarters of a mile to meet a junction of tracks not far from ruined St Andrew's chapel which stands up over the field on the right.

Turn left along another track which passes some carr stone cottages and then Downs Farm on the right. Go through a gateway into Ringstead Downs Nature Reserve. The track through the Downs eventually comes out at the Sedgeford road.

3. Turn left here and passing the gates to Ringstead Hall carry on past a house on the left, then over Hall Lane, bearing right near a pond on the left, to meet a junction of roads. Turn left here (now on the route of the Peddars Way) and continue on past the Gin Trap and art gallery on the right. Avoid all turnings and carry on walking up the High Street, passing the village shop and tearoom, and St Andrew's church. At another road junction (with an arrow marker on a telegraph pole) ignore the road ahead which goes to Hunstanton (possible short cut)

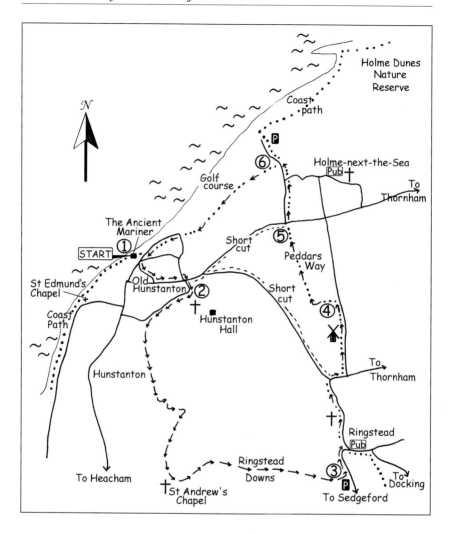

and bear right round the corner still continuing along the Peddars Way.
Shortly, passing some houses on the left, come to another road junction.
The road ahead goes to Thornham, but the route (arrow marker on
telegraph pole) turns left here along Peddars Way North with houses
and a pavement now on the right and Ringstead windmill on the left.

4. At the end of the houses look for a signpost to the left which points
the Peddars Way as a narrow path along a field boundary. At the end of
the field turn right at the arrow marker onto the true route of the

The coast path, Holme-next-the-Sea

Peddars Way. The Way is then lined with trees on either side giving lovely views over Holme, the marshes and the sea. The path comes out onto the main A149 coast road (a second possible short cut turning left) by a bungalow.

5. Cross carefully (look for a wooden signpost) and continue down the lane ahead. Follow the gentle bends of this hedged lane eventually passing scattered housing, and keeping on ahead where a turn to the right by a duckpond leads into Holme village. The Peddars Way eventually passes a car park and toilets, and crosses Hunstanton golf course to the beach. However, some way before the beach, this walk returns along the Coast Path which starts in Hunstanton.

6. Just beyond a small bridge over the river Hun, turn left (wooden signpost) and walk alongside the river, with a caravan site on the right. This is soon left behind as you go through wooden posts and continue on along the river, with the golf course fenced off on the right and the sea kept at bay by dunes beyond. Carry on for some distance (arrow markers) detouring round a small pump building until the track goes

through wooden barriers (arrow marker) to meet a small road by a hotel on the left. Continue ahead along a road which passes the golf clubhouse on the right and continues along a gravelled road (arrow marker on right) passing houses, fences and gardens back to the crossroads near the Le Strange Arms (arrow marker). The lane to the right leads to the lifeboat station, a beach café, toilets and the sea. Carry straight on back to the Ancient Mariner. To reach the start of the Coast Path continue on to the corner and then bear right and left to walk along the cliffs, passing ornamental gardens to reach the green by the sea in the town centre.

 THE NORFOLK COAST PATH – Hunstanton to Thornham (5 miles)

Start at the remains of Hunstanton pier (washed away in 1978) near the bandstand on the central green. With the sea on the left, walk up through the Esplanade Gardens to the café near the bowling greens where there is a large map of the Peddars Way and the Coast Path. Continue along the broad green by the cliff top passing between the lighthouse and the sea with the ruins of the medieval chapel of St Edmund on the right. Carry on along the edge of a car park going through a gap at the end. Here either bear left then right and walk along the beach or go ahead along a narrow path through bushes which wends its way along the back of beach huts (the official Coast Path route). For both routes turn right up a lane past the Inshore Lifeboat House, and just before a crossroads with the Ancient Mariner on the right, bear left along a gravelled lane between houses, eventually coming out at the golf club house on the left. Continue on along the roadway leaving it as it swings right. Go through a gate onto the golf course and follow the line of the little river Hun to a bridge near a caravan site. Turn left down the lane here and continue on to the dunes behind the beach where an arrow marker points the Coast Path to the right, on a path along the edge of a marsh with the golf course on the right. The path continues on to a boarded walk near houses going through Holme Dunes Nature Reserve and Holme Bird Observatory. It then bears right along a sea wall in the direction of Thornham.

THORNHAM, THORNHAM CREEK AND STAITHE
The King's Head
◆❖◆

Springtime is a good season to do this walk when the acid green of the alexanders (a giant type of cow parsley) contrasts with the white blossom of the hedgerows, the burnt gold of new poplar leaves and the fresh red of copper beeches. The walk climbs quiet roads behind Thornham turning back with spectacular views over the marshes to pass through flowery orchards to the Coast Path, which follows a sea wall along boat-filled creeks back to the village.

The beautiful village of Thornham, with its old cottages built mainly of blocks of chalk, has had an interesting history. It was once a flourishing port with granaries and jetties (the old coal barn and some timber piles in the creek are the only remaining signs), but trade was killed off by the advent of the railway to nearby Hunstanton. Then a notable iron working business was started by Mrs Ames Lyde, who made ironwork to grace the royal property at Sandringham. Ironworking is still carried out in the village today. Beautifully worked gates can be seen fronting the early 18th century Red House on the main road. All Saints' church has Early English and Perpendicular work, with lovely carved bench ends.

The King's Head is a pretty-as-a-picture pub occupying a prominent corner site in the centre of Thornham. To one side is a flower-edged lawn with tables shaded by mature trees. To the rear is another beer garden which is fenced off for children. There are two petanque pitches. Dogs are welcome in the garden areas and in the wooden floored bar. There are six bed and breakfast rooms.

The pub is open Monday to Friday from 11.30 am to 3 pm and 6 pm to 11 pm. On Saturday the hours are 11.30 am to 11 pm and on Sunday 12 noon to 10.30 pm (summer). Food is served Monday to Thursday 12 noon to 2 pm and 6.30 pm to 9 pm, Friday 12 noon to 2 pm and 6.30 pm to 9.30 pm, Saturday 12 noon to 2.30 pm and 6.30 pm to 9 pm, Sunday 12 noon to 2.30 pm and 6.30 pm to 9 pm. Real ales are Greene King Abbot and IPA, and Adnam's bitter, with a changing guest beer. Draught lagers are Kronenbourg and Carlsberg, with Guinness on tap, and Strongbow as the cider.

The food is delicious and the choice is from the light menu at lunchtime with such delights as platter of crab, prawns and smoked salmon, to the full menu in the evening which includes serious dishes such as lobster thermidor. Food can be eaten in the cosy bar areas or in the two section restaurant with a cheery red dado and cloths and napkins to match. Telephone: 01485 512213.

- **HOW TO GET THERE:** The King's Head is on the main A149 coast road in the centre of Thornham near the church.
- **PARKING:** Large car park to the side of the pub, or park at the staithe.
- **LENGTH OF THE WALK:** 6¼ miles (with two short cuts). Map: OS Explorer 250 Norfolk Coast West (GR 733434).

THE WALK

1. Leave the pub, cross the main road and walk to the right along it. For a shorter route continue along the main road to reach the track which goes right through orchards. For the main walk, take a left turn, signposted to Ringstead, and walk up the lane. The road rises gently between hedges passing a right turn to Ringstead after about ¾ mile. Use this for a short cut or for the full walk, keep straight on for some distance passing Keeper's Cottage on the left in a wood.

2. Follow the road as it turns to the right where a track goes off left to Lyng Farm. Then where the road veers left, turn right onto a broad grassy track (signpost and arrow marker). Come out at a T-junction (arrow markers) opposite a trig point. Walk down the lane ahead which, after passing an earthwork (a 1st century fort) in the field on the right, meets the main A149 coast road.

3. Cross carefully and go along the broad stony track ahead passing one or two dwellings. The route then goes ahead through a gateway along a wide grassy track through orchards. At another gateway walk left towards a stand of poplars over a little bridge, then shortly right again along a deep ditch. At the end of the poplar wood bear left, then soon right over a wooden bridge (arrow marker) and continue ahead. The path does a little wiggle to the left and right over a tiny plank footbridge (arrow marker).

The marshes at Thornham

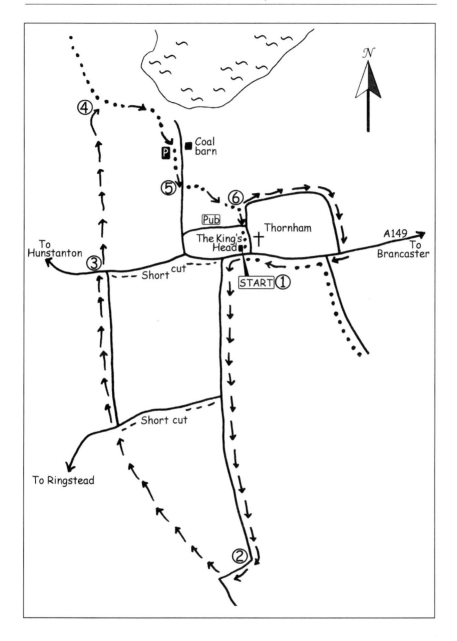

The coal barn, Thornham

4. Go up the bank and onto the Coast Path just by a gate and a Holme Dunes Reserve explanatory board. Turn right along the bank and enjoy the view over the marshes to the sea. Follow the sea wall to the right and go through by another gate whereupon the wall bears left again. A deep creek here has moorings for pleasure and fishing boats. There are complex systems of sluices and drainage channels. Ignore a branch path to a sluice on the left and continue on ahead (arrow marker). The wall then bends left to go towards a picturesque coal barn, then bears right again to border a creek with the road beyond. Go through by another gate and bear left to the lane.

5. Go a little way up the lane, then turn left over a small wooden bridge (arrow marker) onto a narrow path which borders the marsh. Over the fields on the right is the old Lifeboat Inn. Follow the curve of the path which eventually crosses a little bridge to come out onto a cross track. Turn right to meet Church Street. Here the Coast Path turns right.

6. This walk bears left along a lane called The Green passing housing to reach Oldfield Green. Follow the road through the Green and right up Green Lane to meet the main A149 road. Turn right along the pavement here, ignore the left turn signposted to Choseley (which is where the Coast Path leaves the village) and walk through the village of Thornham passing interesting houses and cottages, including the Old School and Schoolhouse. Opposite the church is the green with its village sign and over the side road is the pub.

 THE NORFOLK COAST PATH – Thornham to Brancaster (2⅔ miles)

The Coast Path continues up Church Lane turning left just past the church to go along the main A149 coast road through the village, taking the first turn on the right signposted to Choseley. Walk up this lane for about a mile turning left at a clump of trees to walk along the edge of fields. Cross over one road leading down to Titchwell and at a second road join the route of the next walk.

BRANCASTER, THE BEACH, GIPSY LANE AND BRANODUNUM
The Ship Inn
⋯⋄⋄⋯

This lovely walk does a loop through marshes to the sea and then climbs the easy hill behind Brancaster to meet the Coast Path, which here passes through gently undulating farmland. The route then continues on through Branodunum, site of an important Roman fort. On your way, look for signs of coastal erosion - the sea is threatening to sweep back to its former line much nearer to the old settlements along the coast.

Brancaster is a delightful village full of old and interesting houses and cottages, popular with holidaymakers. Branodunum, to the east, is the site of an important Roman shore fort. It belongs to the National Trust as does Scolt Head, the mysterious constantly shifting island just offshore, and 17th century Dial House, at nearby Brancaster Staithe. The staithe was famous for whelk fishing, but now fishing has taken rather a back seat, though there is a faithful sailing clientele when the tide is high.

Titchwell is a hamlet on the edge of marshes with a popular RSPB reserve 2 miles to the west. Its tiny church of St Mary has a round Norman tower and there is an ancient pillar or wayside cross on the main road.

In common with many of the pubs in this locality, the Ship, dating back to the 1700s, has links with Lord Nelson, who lived in nearby Burnham Thorpe. He often visited his nanny, Mrs Blackett, who retired here to live with her son, the landlord. There is a splendid 100 year old replica of a man o' war of Nelson's days on the outside wall. Inside there is a traditional bar and a large non-smoking restaurant which can seat 40+ people. To the side is a pleasant walled beer garden. The pub offers bed and breakfast in four en suite rooms, including one family one. The menu is based on traditional pub food with jacket potatoes, sandwiches and ploughman's available at lunchtime. Children are especially well catered for with six choices on their menu. Chef's specials are written up on a board and often include fresh seafood. There are usually five or six vegetarian options. Real ales on offer are Greene King IPA and Abbott with Foster's, Kronenbourg and Carlsberg lagers. The draught cider is Strongbow.

Opening hours are 12 noon to 3 pm and 7 pm to 11 pm. Sunday closing is 10.30 pm. Food is served from 12 noon to 2 pm (2.30 pm weekends) and from 7 pm to 9 pm (from 6 pm in summer). Hours are often extended during the summer months. Telephone: 01485 210333.

- **HOW TO GET THERE:** The pub is on the A149 coast road in the middle of Brancaster opposite the church. Brancaster is half way between Hunstanton and Wells-next-the-Sea.
- **PARKING:** Plenty of parking to the rear and to the side of the pub. There is also a beach car park near the golf club.
- **LENGTH OF THE WALK**: 6 miles (with two short cuts). Map: OS Explorer 250 Norfolk Coast West (GR 773438).

THE WALK

1. Leave the Ship and cross the road, turning left to walk along the pavement passing St Mary's church. At the crossroads, turn right to walk down Broad Lane signposted to the beach. This is part of the Coast Path. Cross over Butcher's Lane on the right. The road narrows to a

St Mary's church, Titchwell

gateway before it goes through the marsh. Just before this turn left (leaving the route of the Coast Path) along a track to reach some iron railings just past a bungalow on the right. Turn right through these and follow the signposted path to the beach passing a wartime pill box and continuing on along a sea wall, following the line of the road through the marshes towards the golf clubhouse ahead. If the tide is low you can cross a stile and come down off the bank to the right near public conveniences and continue ahead through the gap between the golf clubhouse and the golf course on to Brancaster beach, passing an explanatory board erected by the National Trust.

2. Turn left along the beach for a fairly short distance to reach a track which goes inland at the end of the sea defences, passing over a recently built drainage sluice. If the tide is high and you cannot go through the gap continue along the bank which bears left and then comes down to a fenced-off path between the dunes and the golf practice green. This meets Gipsy Lane, a track from the beach which starts as a boarded walk and turns left to go inland initially as a bank through marshes (signpost). The bank veers to the right and then turning sharp left becomes a tree-

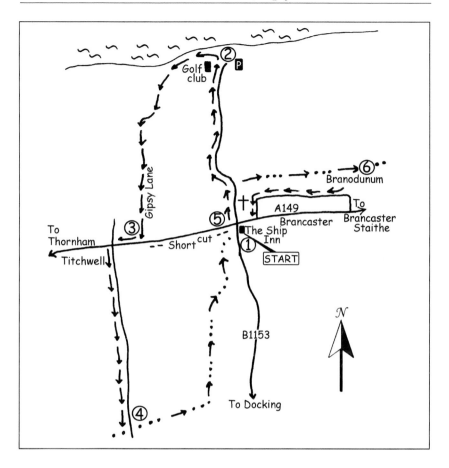

lined lane passing between fields to reach the main A149 coast road. A left turn here offers a short cut back to Brancaster.

3. For the full walk, turn right along the pavement and walk into Titchwell village. At the crossroads where an ancient pillar stands, it is worth turning right to look at St Mary's church with its round Norman tower. To continue the walk, take a left turn at the crossroads and follow a small lane uphill. At the brow of the hill where the lane narrows there is a cross track.

4. Turn left here to join the Coast Path (look for the arrow marker and signpost). After about half a mile it reaches a cross track (arrow marker) where the Coast Path turns left down towards

Brancaster Marsh

Brancaster. This is another broad track which passes the buildings of School Farm on the right. The track veers to the right and left again to reach the outskirts of Brancaster where it becomes metalled near a 30 mph sign. After modern housing, it bears rightish to pass between some old cottages just before it comes out onto the Docking road opposite the village shop. The walk can be shortened here by turning right along the main A149 road to return to the Ship. However it is well worth doing another short loop along the Coast Path to the site of the ancient fort of Branodunum.

5. To do this cross the A149 and go ahead down Broad Lane leading to the beach again. Instead of turning left as before carry on just past the gates leading on to the marsh and turn right here (signposted) along a small reed-fringed path which leads alongside the marsh, often on a board walk as the ground can be very soggy. Avoid the two footpaths signposted to the right and carry on over a metal stile (arrow marker). After about half a mile, at the end of the houses, watch out for a stile with an explanatory board nearby. This gives historical details of the Branodunum site.

6. Leave the Coast Path here and turn right over the stile and go straight across the field on a permissive footpath to a wooden gate on the other side. Cross a stile which leads on to a lane at a corner. Turn right down Cross Lane to a T-junction. Turn right down a broad signposted track towards the marsh for a short distance and then turn left along another signposted footpath which goes through fencing across fields. This comes out between houses via iron railings onto London Street. Turn left up the road to meet the main A149 road again. A short distance to the right is the pub.

 THE NORFOLK COAST PATH – Branodunum to Norton Marshes (3¾ miles)

The Coast Path carries on from the Branodunum site alongside the marshes crossing a stile near Brancaster Staithe where it continues past the back of a huge converted malt house, skirting left behind Dial House on the right along a small path which emerges onto the staithe. Cross the hard and continue on along a narrow track passing the Sailing Club on the right. The path continues along the edge of the marsh (this may be muddy and under water at high tide) to cross a stony track which leads up to the Jolly Sailors pub. It then goes through a passage between whelk sheds a little to the right and carries on between the edges of creeks and the grounds of houses to reach the raised bank at Burnham Deepdale. The Coast Path curves along this bank which skirts round Deepdale and Norton Marshes to meet the route of the next circular walk from Burnham Market.

THE FOUR BURNHAMS –
BURNHAM MARKET, NORTON,
OVERY STAITHE AND OVERY TOWN

The Hoste Arms

*It is difficult to imagine a more attractive small town than Burnham
Market with its grand Georgian houses and pretty cottages clustering
round a large green. This walk starts here and links several of the seven
Burnhams as well as following a drove road out onto the marshes,
teeming with bird life and rewarding the walker with wide views out to
sea and Scott Head Island. A truly magical walk through a landscape full
of history.*

The beautiful small town of Burnham Market, with its splendid green
backed by Georgian houses and cottages, includes three of the seven
Burnhams (Ulph, Sutton and Westgate). The church of St Mary's,

Westgate, with its fine flint tower, stands near 18th century Westgate Hall, whereas All Saints' Ulph church is at the other end of Burnham Market and Sutton church is in ruins. The fascinating church of St Margaret, Burnham Norton, meanwhile, stands in a commanding position on the hillside overlooking Norton village and the marshes. St Mary's church at Burnham Deepdale on the main road has a Saxon round tower and a Norman font. Interesting St Clement's at Burnham Overy Town is 13th century with a square central tower and bell turret, and All Saints' at Burnham Thorpe to the southeast, the birthplace of Nelson, is also 13th century and contains items associated with the great seaman. Just outside Burnham Market is the splendid 15th century gatehouse of St Mary's Carmelite friary.

The cheerful yellow-painted Hoste Arms, now an upmarket restaurant and hotel with 36 rooms, still has an old-fashioned bar strictly dedicated to drinking. Formerly a manor house, in 1651 a relation of William Pitt opened the building as a coaching inn called the Pitt Arms. In 1811 it was renamed the Hoste Arms after Captain Sir William Hoste, one of Nelson's protégés, who owned nearby Sandringham. Now privately owned, it has been stripped back as far as possible to its original old brick walls and floors and decorated with panache. Food is taken very seriously at the Hoste and there are several areas for eating. The conservatory lounge, which leads into a covered patio/garden with tables, is used for morning coffee, afternoon tea and light lunches. It has smoking and non-smoking areas. Otherwise, meals can be eaten in the Front Room (decorated with a series of exquisite local watercolours), the Music Room, or the two sophisticated red and tartan dining rooms.

The brasserie menu, which changes every five weeks, is comprehensive and imaginative – you can have anything from a sandwich through to very tempting starters and main meals with an emphasis on fish, to puddings which are just that bit different. Seared tuna, pak choy, ginger and lemongrass sounds delicious, as does one of the vegetarian options – mushroom, spinach and parmesan risotto with rocket salad. To complement the food, there is an extensive wine list. Real ales are Woodforde's Wherry, Greene King IPA and Abbot, plus guest beers. Draught lagers are Kronenbourg and Carlsberg, and there is always a draught cider. The bar is open from 11 am to 11 pm with Sunday hours of 12 noon to 10.30 pm. Lunch is served from 12 noon to 2 pm and dinner from 7 pm to 9 pm. Breakfast is from 7.30 am to 10.30 am and afternoon tea from 3 pm to 5.45 pm. Telephone: 01328 738777.

The 15th century friary gatehouse of St Mary's

- **How to get there:** The Hoste Arms overlooks one end of the green in the centre of Burnham Market which is just a few miles south of Burnham Overy Staithe on the A149 coast road.
- **Parking:** Behind the pub; in front on the green, or on the hard at Burnham Overy Staithe.
- **Length of the walk:** 6½ miles (with several opportunities for short cuts). Map: OS Explorer 251 Norfolk Coast Central (GR 831422).

The Walk

1. Turn left out of the Hoste Arms, then very shortly turn left again up a narrow lane lined with houses and cottages, old and new. At the end of the houses, a green lane called Cross Lane leads to the right to Burnham Norton church and another lane goes to the left, but keep on the road a little longer until it bears to the right. For a short cut keep on along the road, turning right onto the A149 coast road into Burnham Overy Staithe.

2. For the main walk through lovely marshes take a signposted footpath to the left along the edge of a field with a hedge on the left. Follow this path where the view opens out over Burnham Norton, the marshes and sea, and to Burnham Overy windmill on the right. When the hedge ends at another footpath signpost, continue rightish along a baulk between two fields towards a bus shelter on the main road.

Cross the coast road (A149) and go down the lane opposite to Burnham Norton. Follow along the old wall of a farmhouse on the left. Pass a telephone box, and another gaggle of cottages. The lane bears round to the left. Bear right near a public footpath signpost along a track between the marsh and an old flint house. Just beyond this a signpost points straight on to Burnham Overy Staithe and a short cut can be taken by following this.

3. To continue the main walk bear left (signposted to the Coast Path); go through two lots of gates and on along a broad track curving through the marshes crisscrossed with channels of water and teeming with bird life. The windmill and cottages of Burnham Overy Staithe stand up over the marshes on the right. The wind whips across here and the reeds flutter like prayer flags. The track does a little loop to right and left and follows a deep dyke on the left. The broad track bends slightly to the left. Here the right of way goes over a stile and across a marshy field but it is probably better to stick to the broad track which continues on still

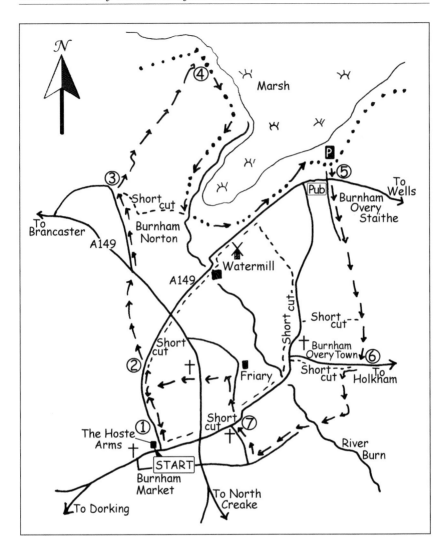

with a deep dyke on the left. When this ends continue following the line of the fence on the right, going over a small bridge by a gate and up onto the sea wall built in 1821 to defend the grazing marsh from the sea. From here there are lovely views over to Scolt Head Island, an important nature reserve.

  4. Turn right along the wall heading in the direction of Burnham Overy Staithe. A creek bears left to run past the quay there.

The church at Burnham Overy

Continue on to where the bank bears sharp left just where the short cut, a footpath from Burnham Norton, joins it. There is a web of dykes and sluices here to control the water and the tides. Cross a stile by a wooden gate and go slightly to the left across the middle of a field towards the windmill. There is a footpath on the left but no access to Burnham Overy Staithe from it. This is still the Coast Path and at the road provision has been made to walk inside the hedge to reach Burnham Overy Staithe. A track signposted to the right over the road provides another short cut to Burnham Overy Town and thence to Burnham Market. The main walk continues on coming out onto a pavement leading into Burnham Overy Staithe, once a sizeable port and now an attractive waterside village. A ferry runs during the summer months to Scolt Head Island National Nature Reserve. Turn left down West Harbour Way and follow the road alongside the creek passing the boathouse and ship's chandlery on the right.

5. The Coast Path swings left at the end of the hard to follow a bank towards the sea. This walk bears right up East Harbour Way passing the house of Admiral Woodget of the *Cutty Sark* on the right. At the top, cross the main road and continue on up Gong Lane. When the houses end this becomes a lovely wide green lane hedged on either side. Continue on as the lane does a little wiggle. Pass a broad green lane to the right – yet another short cut via Burnham Overy Town.

6. For the main walk, continue on to the road and turn right for a short distance passing houses. The road is another short cut to Burnham Market but for the main, and more interesting walk, go to the left at the end of the houses along a narrow signposted footpath along the edge of a field, making for woods ahead. At the strip of woodland, bear left along a small but obvious path up onto an old railway embankment. Turn right along this, walking through woodland with a marshy area on the left (osier carr). Cross over the little River Burn and pass a sewage works, coming out onto the road leading to the works. Carry on ahead along this road until it comes out at a crossroads. Turn right here along tiny Joan Short's lane to a T-junction on the outskirts of Burnham Market.

7. The direct route back to the pub turns left here. However, it is well worth turning right, then shortly afterwards left again to go down Friar's Lane to the remains of St Mary's Carmelite friary. To rejoin the walk, go back to a track just before the school which runs left to meet Bellamy's Lane. Turn right here and then very shortly left to go along a track by St Margaret's church, Burnham Norton. The track from the church meets the road taken on the outward journey. Turn left along it back to the pub.

 THE NORFOLK COAST PATH – Burnham Overy to Holkham Gap (4 miles)

This is one of the loveliest sections of the Coast Path. From Burnham Overy Hard take the sea wall which bears left heading towards the sea. Follow it as it bends several times to come out onto the dunes near Gun Hill on the left. The line of the Coast Path is undefined here. Depending on the weather either walk to the right along the beach or go through or alongside the pinewoods in the same direction. After nearly 2 miles look for the break in the pine trees where the main boardwalk access onto Holkham beach from Lady Ann's Drive comes in.

HOLKHAM BEACH, WELLS QUAY, HOLKHAM HALL AND LAKE

The Victoria

This walk is brimful of history - a lively harbour, a great house and park with its lake and monument, the interesting church of St Withburga, and an estate village. The walk begins down Lady Ann's Drive leading to the sea, then passes through woods, where on a warm day the air is scented with pine, honeysuckle and dog roses. A sea wall links the beach with the little port of Wells. From Wells a drive enters the Holkham estate to take the walker round the hall and through lovely woodland and parkland with deer.

It is fortunate that the Coke family still live at Holkham, and that the estate is still run in much the same way as it always was, allowing an excellent balance between farming and wildlife with the beauty of the

Hall, lake and deer park at the centre. Generous public access is allowed to the park. The great Palladian house, designed by William Kent, has awe-inspiring interiors. In the grounds are a triumphal archway, St Withburga's church restored in 1870, and the great obelisk monument to Coke of Norfolk, the agricultural reformer, as well as an interesting ice house. Holkham village cottages line the entrance drive, with a pottery, shop and tea room in the Ancient House and a Bygones exhibition and Stables Café at the Hall. Holkham Nursery Garden is enclosed in the huge walls of the old vegetable garden, with its orangery at the entrance. The pine woodlands by the sea, now part of a huge National Nature Reserve, were planted in the mid 19th century as protection from the wind and waves.

The woods link Holkham with the beach and marshland at Wells-next-the-Sea. This interesting port still has a small fishing fleet. St Nicholas church, rebuilt after fire in 1879, is surrounded by interesting old streets. There is a small Maritime Museum in the old Lifeboat House.

The Victoria hotel, now run by the Holkham estate, is a solid flint, Grade II listed, former coaching inn built to celebrate the birth of Queen Victoria. Its exterior is rather austere, but inside is a riot of colour. The public rooms are decorated with an Indian theme – wooden furniture in the restaurant and colourful squashy sofas and cushions in the lounge warmed by a roaring log fire. The residents' lounge is in a more sober English style, but still warm and comfortable (there are 11 bedrooms). There are fine views over the marshes.

The Victoria serves breakfast, lunch, afternoon tea and dinner. The food is upmarket and delicious, ranging from simple bar grub, which is replaced by a barbecue in summer, through a lunch menu which includes terrine of Holkham game with plum chutney to a dinner menu which offers chargrilled fillet of Holkham beef. The menu also features game birds and venison in season, all from the Holkham estate. The menus are changed frequently.

Adnam's beers and Woodforde's Wherry are on draught all the time, with interesting guest ales such as Buffy's Folly. Various lagers are on draught and there is an excellent wine list and wines by the glass. The hotel is open all day every day and food is served from 12 noon to 2.30 pm and from 7 pm to 9.30 pm Monday to Friday with longer serving hours at the weekend. Dogs are allowed in the black and red tiled Holkham tap bar. Telephone: 01328 711008.

- **How to get there:** The Victoria at Holkham is on the main A149 coast road between Wells and Burnham Overy Staithe.
- **Parking:** To the side of the pub or in Lady Ann's Drive.
- **Length of the walk:** 8½ miles (with several opportunities for short cuts). Map: OS Explorer 251 Norfolk Coast Central (GR 891440).

The Walk

1. Leave the Victoria and cross the A149 coast road carefully. Walk ahead down Lady Ann's Drive through an avenue of poplar trees with grazing marshes on either side. The drive ends at white gates by a belt of pine trees. Go through the gate to a walkway leading through to the beach and sea. (You can go along this and turn right walking along the beach to eventually reach the lifeboathouse at Wells.)

2. However, the official track of the Coast Path (which is arrow marked) bears to the right before the walkway and follows a broad sandy track between pine woods and a fringe of trees bordering grazing marshes. Go through by a gate and continue on for about a mile and a half. Various tracks go to the left through the woods to the beach and in parts the track passes through more open areas of sandy heath dotted with silver birch trees. Leave the seclusion of the pine woods to reach the caravan park near the beach at Wells. A broad drove road starts at a gate to the right of the caravan park. Ignore this and bear left alongside a small lake. Go through a gap by a wooden gate. Follow the direction of an arrow marker to the right and continue on to another small gate with an arrow marker. Steps lead up through the pines to the beach on the left. Ignore these and go ahead along the edge of a car park towards a beach café. Go in front of the café and a set of wooden steps takes the Coast Path up onto the sea wall. The gaily painted lifeboat station is on the left standing guard over the channel which leads into Wells harbour.

3. Turn right and walk down the path towards Wells with views of moored boats and marshes. Continue on past Wells Maritime Museum. A map of the Peddars Way and the Coast Path is on the wall of the sea defences opposite toilets. The quay on the left is still used by ships trading in animal feeds and fertilisers.

4. Turn right, leaving the route of the Coast Path, and continue on along a street called The Quay, passing shops, restaurants and

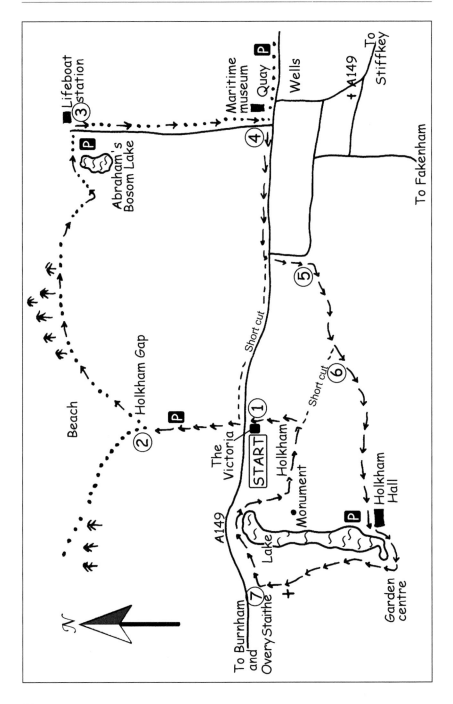

The Harbour and Quay at Wells-next-the-Sea

interesting old cottages. Eventually the buildings end, the road passes through the remains of an old railway bridge and meets a crossroad. For a short cut bear right and follow the main road back to the pub. For the full walk, turn left and walk up a short stretch of the main road to the corner. Here the road veers sharply to the left.

5. Take the broad drive to the right which is lined with gnarled holm oak trees. Go through a wicket gate by a larger metal gate marked 'Walkers Only', by a Gothic windowed lodge into the grounds of Holkham Hall. The Earl of Leicester kindly allows walkers to use the paths through the park during daylight hours. Please be especially careful to shut all gates because of the livestock. Continue along this drive through trees to an intersection of paths. A track to the right through trees affords a short cut to Holkham village and the North Gates which gives access to the pub. However it is well worthwhile extending the walk through this delightful park in the creation of which three famous designers, William Kent, Capability Brown and Humphrey Repton, have had a hand.

6. To do this continue along the main track ahead which passes

The ice house at Holkham House

through farm fields dotted with parkland trees and backed by woods. A track comes in from the left, but continue to follow the main track as it veers to the right and goes over a cattlegrid to enter the park proper, grazed by sheep and dotted with huge mature trees. The top of a monument pokes out of trees. A farm track comes in from the left by a wood and a little further on the main route for cars entering by the North Gates joins at an intersection from the right. Continue straight on through a gate by a cattle grid, ignore the track leading to the estate office and pottery on the left and carry on ahead to pass through a parking area under the trees.

Take the opportunity to visit this grand 18th-century Palladian mansion (open on Bank Holidays and daily in the afternoon, except Friday and Saturday, from June to the end of September). Then follow the drive as it veers to the left round the Hall. At the end of the lake turn off the main drive and go down a branch leading to the right signposted to the garden centre. On a mound to the left can be seen the redbrick 17th-century ice house. The small roadway leading to the garden centre goes over a cattle grid fenced on either side. A little way before this follow a grassy track to the right through trees towards the end of the lake. On the left before a metal gate ahead is a wooden gate. Go through this and turn to the right to go through another gate (metal this time) and follow the broad grassy track which leads in the general direction of the church. The track passes St Withburga's church set on a mound surrounded by trees. Shortly after the church the track makes for Church Lodge which stands guardian to gates in the estate wall leading onto the A149 road.

7. Just before this turn right along another broad track which passes a small barn on the left and goes through woods alive with deer. The track curves round the end of the lake passing through a metal gate. Keep ahead at a junction of tracks where the lake ends, to walk through more woods. The track veers sharply to the left where a smaller track approaches the monument on the right (this was erected in 1845 as a tribute to Coke of Norfolk). Continue along the main track which leads eventually to Holkham estate village. Go through a small gate (North Gates) by a cattlegrid and turn left to walk down the village street, back to the Victoria.

 THE NORFOLK COAST PATH – Wells to Warham Greens (1 mile)

Turn left to walk along Wells quay, then when the main road turns sharp right, continue straight on along a creekside lane jammed with interesting houses and cottages. Pass Wells Sailing Club and then when the road ends, go ahead bearing slightly to the left through fishermen's shacks and continue on, without turning off, onto a sea wall which curves through the marshes. Follow the bank as it bears right to join the route of the next walk at the beginning of Warham Greens.

WARHAM, WELLS AND WARHAM SALT MARSH

The Three Horseshoes

A walk which combines views of the sea and the delights of the salt marshes with some fascinating snippets of history associated with the pretty and interesting village of Warham near the river Stiffkey. Warham camp, a quarter of a mile from the village, is an Iron Age fort linked to the Iceni tribe with two circles of earthworks and magnificent views, while the two churches and the remains of a third testify to the village's importance in the Middle Ages.

Warham is a scattered village consisting of the pub, a few cottages and the nearby church of All Saints at a crossroads, with the church of Warham St Mary's, together with a few houses and a farm to the east. A mile to the south, in a bend of the river Stiffkey, are the splendid embankments of Iron Age Warham Camp, associated with the Iceni tribe and their queen, Boudicca who led a revolt against the Romans in AD 60.

Visiting the Three Horseshoes is like stepping back in time to the 1920s. There is gas lighting, pine panelling, old furniture, flyscreening at the windows, and all sorts of old kitchen, dairy and wash house utensils, china, old posters, at least one grandfather clock, stuffed birds and a pianola. Plants spill from all sorts of containers as well as fresh flowers.

The landlord is renowned for his good food as several of the diners I met were keen to underline. It has meant that the pub is often bursting at the seams. The accent is on seriously good food à la Mrs Beeton, made on the premises using fresh local produce. The daily selection on the blackboards above the fireplace in the main bar could include imaginative soups, Mrs Beeton's potted cheese or Warham rabbit casserole. All the starters are unusual and interesting: the main dishes have a local flavour and various fish dishes appear. The puddings are traditional, often with a slightly different twist, and snacks such as sandwiches, ploughman's and jacket potatoes are available. Children can have smaller portions at a reduced price but there are no chips.

The quality of the beer complements the food. Real ales are served straight from the barrel and drip into jerry pots on old milking stools. There is Woodforde's Wherry, Greene King Abbot and IPA, Mardley's Mild and a guest beer – something like Woodforde's Nelson's Revenge. On draught are Murphy's stout, Dry Blackthorn cider and Carlsberg Export lager. The pub also offers Whin Hill, a local medium dry cider as well as home-made lemonade and ginger beer. Wine comes in small bottles as well as large and a range of fruit wines is available.

The pub is open every day from 11.30 am to 2.30 pm and from 6 pm to 11 pm (10.30 pm on Sundays). Food is served from 12 noon to 1.45 pm and from 6 pm to 8.30 pm. There are two gardens and accommodation is available. Dogs are welcome. Telephone: 01328 710547

- **HOW TO GET THERE:** The Three Horseshoes is on a crossroads in the centre of Warham. The village is not far from Wells on a turning off the B1105 which goes from Wells to Little Walsingham and Fakenham.
- **PARKING:** There is ample car parking in a field over the road from the pub or limited parking at the end of the lane leading to the marsh.
- **LENGTH OF THE WALK:** 5¼ miles (with one short cut). Map: OS Explorer 251 Norfolk Coast Central (GR 948417). The marshes can be muddy or under water at especially high tides so take care.

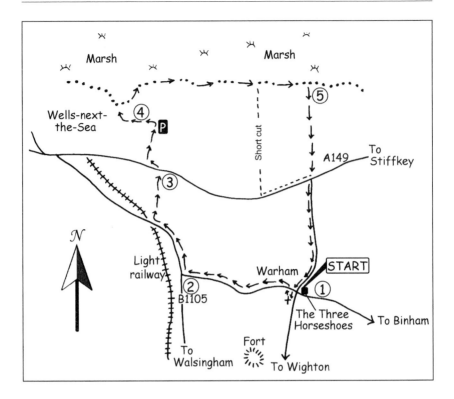

THE WALK

1. Leave the Three Horseshoes and go straight up the lane ahead for a detour which leads to the pretty church of All Saints and further on to the fort on the right.

For the main walk, turn right out of the pub and go over the crossroads along the road passing some interesting old buildings. A brick and flint wall on the right leads on to the entrance to another church (St Mary Magdalen) with a little dressed flint porch with a sun dial and small flint tower. Continue on from the church passing lovely old houses and farms. Follow the road as it bends to the left and reaches a crossroads.

2. Turn right here along the B1105 Wells to Walsingham road. This can be busy in summer but there is a reasonable verge to walk along with views of the sea ahead. Just before the bridge over the Wells to Walsingham railway, there is a track to the right marked by a wooden signpost. Walk along this broad stony track aiming straight at the sea.

Warham Iron Age fort

There are hedges on either side. Keep ahead near concrete hard standing opposite some mellow old barns. The views are of the marshes, the pinewoods and the lifeboat station at Wells beach. The track meets the main A149 coast road.

3. Turn left for a little way along it and just where the road widens out, turn right down a broad stony track (signposted) heading for the sea. Where the hedges end bear slightly to the left and carry on ahead through dikes. There is a parking area just here. Climb the stile to the left of a metal gate and carry on along a broad green ride to the left alongside a dike on the left. The green lane veers to the right and goes towards a high sea wall.

4. Climb up this steep bank to join the Coast Path and bear right along it to a small gate (with an arrow marker). Beyond this a narrow path leads on through a copse and scrub and emerges near the marsh. Bear right along a broad green ride along the edge of the marsh. Here and there are rotted hulks of old boats and bridges lead further out into the marsh. The track narrows and bears to the right round a soggy area. Skirt round this bearing to the left and then continue on past a marshy pond on the left. The track goes over a hump and continues on passing some mature trees. On the far, far horizon the old lifeboat station at Blakeney Point sticks up over the marsh. Up the slope on the right is a gate which leads to Garden Drove track (a short cut) and on the left a track leads out onto the marsh over a footbridge. This is Warham Saltmarsh Nature Reserve, part of Holkham National Nature Reserve.

Continue on along the edge of the marsh following the broad green ride. Barns punctuate the horizon on the right. Go through a metal gate by an old pit and continue on. By another notice about wildfowling and Warham saltmarsh, a stony track heads out into the marsh. The green ride widens out into a broad green area just here where this walk leaves the Coast Path.

5. On the right is a metal gate with a small gate next to it. Go through this and continue on up a broad, hedged, stony track (Cocklestrand Drove). The track does a little wiggle as it approaches the road (signposted). Cross the main coast road carefully and go up the lane on the other side. Pass the drive leading to Northgate Hall Farm on the right and continue on to the outskirts of the village of Warham. As you pass housing on the right, the lane (Stiffkey Road) bends to the right. Go on into Chapel Street and continue on back to the pub

 THE NORFOLK COAST PATH – Warham Marsh to Stiffkey (1½ miles)

To follow the coast path continue on along the marshes past the end of Cocklestrand Drove for over a mile to reach a lane which turns inland to Stiffkey. Continue on along the edge of the marshes to reach Hollow Lane where the walk from Stiffkey joins the Coast Path.

STIFFKEY, MORSTON GREENS AND COCKTHORPE

The Red Lion

Exhilarating views of sea and marshes dominate most of this walk, whilst inland the views are of woods punctuated by the towers of numerous churches. The return route winds gently down to the village of Stiffkey, an exceptionally pretty mixture of cottages and grand houses in a variety of different local materials.

The pretty river Stiffkey runs through the village of the same name and attractive flint and brick houses and cottages line its bank. Stiffkey cockles (Stewkey blues) from the sand flats out in the National Trust marshes were once famed throughout the land. Just as famous was the early 20th century rector who was defrocked for associating with prostitutes in the guise of helping them. In the 1930s, the author Henry

Williamson tried his hand at farming in Stiffkey at Old Castle Farm. The Perpendicular church of St John the Baptist, which contains a fine monument to Sir Nathaniel Bacon, who built Stiffkey Hall in 1578, is unusual in having the ruins of another church, St Mary's, in its churchyard. Just beyond the church is Tudor Stiffkey Hall and associated ruins. Up on the hillside sits the hamlet of Cockthorpe renowned as the birthplace of Admiral Sir Cloudesley Shovell, a contemporary of Nelson.

A relaxed atmosphere pervades the Red Lion and well-behaved children and dogs are welcome. The main bar has an old red tiled floor and low beams with a huge inglenook fireplace from which warmth radiates in winter and there are plenty of games, newspapers and books to while away time with a drink. Along a corridor and up steps is an impressive dining or function room with a beamed ceiling and boarded floor and an amazing fireplace topped with an antlered deer's head. Next door is a conservatory which leads out onto a pleasant yard with tables and, further, up some steps a small beer garden overlooking the pretty river Stiffkey.

The Red Lion is run on traditional lines and is a beer drinker's mecca with a large variety of real ales and an emphasis on local breweries. When I visited the choice was Winter's Golden, Adnam's Best, Abbot and Woodforde's Wherry. Other beers are introduced according to season. Carlsberg and Budvar are the lagers on tap with Guinness and Aspall cider. There is a good wine list.

Food is served from 12 noon to 2 pm and from 6.30 pm to 9 pm (7 pm in winter). All the food is cooked fresh and will change often according to season and whim. The emphasis is on fish and shellfish which is mostly local. The Blakeney whitebait is excellent as is the crab. Herring roes are a popular snack in winter along with other fish, particularly Stiffkey fish pie. Norfolk duck, with ratatouille, tempts the meat eaters. The pub is open from 12 noon to 2.30 pm and from 6.30 pm to 11 pm with shorter Sunday hours. It opens half an hour later in winter, and maybe half an hour earlier during the summer season. Telephone: 01328 830552.

- **HOW TO GET THERE:** Stiffkey is on the A149 coast road between Wells-next-the-Sea and Sheringham. The pub is on the main road near the centre of the village.
- **PARKING:** There is plenty of room in the car park behind the pub and down Bangay Green Way.
- **LENGTH OF THE WALK:** 6½ miles (with several opportunities for short cuts). Maps: OS Explorer 251 Norfolk Coast Central (GR 968434).

THE WALK

1. Turn left out of the pub and walk carefully along the busy main A149 road passing attractive cottages. Just past the lamp shop, turn left up a narrow lane (Hollow Lane) which leads past the recreation ground and then goes through fields passing a couple of houses on the left to meet a strip of woodland (Coneyford Plantation) bordering the marshes. If it is windy there is a path through the woods which is more sheltered, but the true line of the Coast Path is between the woodland and the marshes.

2. Turn right along the Coast Path. Soon another track comes down to the marshes from the village (Bangay Green Way) but ignore it unless a short cut is needed and continue on along the sandy/ grassy track.

Stiffkey salt marshes on the left are delightful – a puzzle of creeks and pools, glinting blue on a sunny day at high tide, purple with sea lavender in the summer. Beyond the marsh in the distance are the sandy hills and the old lifeboat station on Blakeney Point with a boat-filled creek between. (Blakeney Point, a wildlife reserve on a shingle spit, is accessible only by a three mile walk or by boat from Blakeney or Morston.) At the marsh edge, the Coast Path meanders through thickets of yellow gorse. It bears right, towards a private track coming down to the marsh and then bears left again to continue following the marsh edge going up onto a bank for some distance. Steps lead down to yet another path approaching the marsh, but ignore this (unless for a short cut back to the village along the busy main road) and continue on.

3. The path now borders Freshes Creek harbouring moored boats. Go through by a gate and bear left round the edge of a creek; the path then bears round to the right again coming onto Morston Greens. The towers of Blakeney church can be glimpsed rising from the trees ahead. Come to an open grassy area where boats are parked and bear round to the right. The path meanders away from the water and goes through a rather muddy patch by some fencing. Soon after, there is a junction of paths; one goes off to the left but this walk goes on to join a path which runs alongside a fence. Carry on along this broad well-used track to meet a cross track. Turn right here and carry on alongside a high bank on the left and a ditch on the right with a jumble of boats in front of an attractive pantiled house.

Just before the house, the Coast Path follows steps up the bank but the walk continues on along the lane, ignoring a path near a National Trust sign to come out on the A149 road.

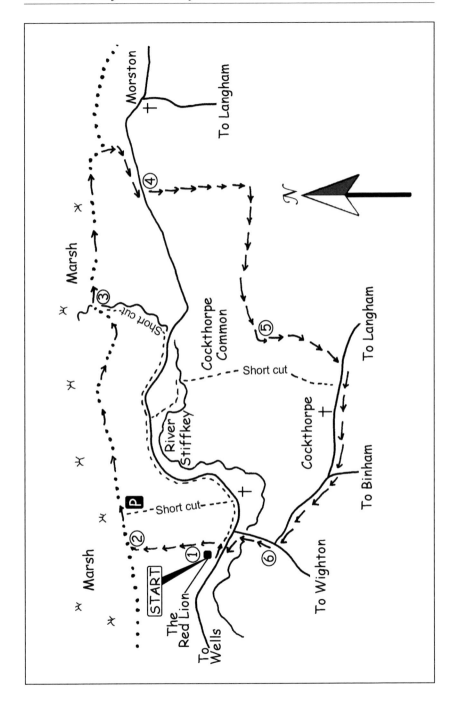

Stiffkey Hall, seen from the churchyard

4. Turn right and walk carefully along the verge for a fairly short distance. Look out for a signposted path which goes off to the left. Go through a small gate by a farm gate to get onto this green track (Love Lane) which goes gently uphill between fields. Look back at the lovely view over Morston church and the marsh and sea. To the left, a house stands high on Blakeney Downs with Blakeney church poking up beyond that, and Langham church lies ahead. Ignore all tracks to left and right and continue on up the hill. Follow the track as it turns to the right on the brow of the hill. Where the track bears sharply to the left carry straight on along a green track with a hedge on the left behind which are some barns and old airfield buildings. The track reaches a cross track. Continue on ahead by a footpath arrow marker over a cultivated field towards another arrow marker on a post at a field boundary. Go ahead over this bigger cultivated field to a post on the other side. There are wide views to the left over a field to a conifer wood and down on the right to the marsh and sea.

5. Turn left up a good track with a view of Cockthorpe village and church. Pass farm buildings on the left. Turn right down a concrete

The river at Stiffkey

cross track passing a conifer wood to meet the road (signpost). Turn right along the road passing Cockthorpe Hall, once the home of Admiral Sir Cloudesley Shovell. Soon on the right a sign points to Cockthorpe Common which is a deep coombe splitting the land (an interesting short cut). This walk continues on past the church of All Saints and along the hedged lane out of Cockthorpe. Ignore a small turning to the left and carry on winding gently downhill towards Stiffkey.

6. Just outside the village a road goes left to Warham and Wighton. Ignore this and bear right down Bridge Street into Stiffkey and its attractive cobbled houses and barns. Cross over the pretty river and go up to the main A149 road again. Turn left along this taking great care as it is very narrow and busy through the village. Pass the shop on the left and then a house on the right marked with a blue plaque (Henry Williamson of *Tarka the Otter* fame lived here). Pass a former chapel now an antiques centre, and continue on past the lamp shop back to the pub.

THE NORFOLK COAST PATH – Morston to Blakeney (1½ miles)

The Coast Path continues near Morston Hard passing the National Trust Information Centre and then weaves gently along the sea wall towards Blakeney. There is a gentle loop past the Red House to reach Blakeney Quay.

CLEY-NEXT-THE-SEA, GLANDFORD, THE RIVER GLAVEN AND BLAKENEY

The George

❧❀❧

This walk, based on the two attractive villages of Cley and Blakeney, is stuffed full of interest. Cley has alleyways lined with ancient cottages, an 18th-century custom house, a picturesque windmill and an exceptional church, while Blakeney offers a 13th-century guildhall undercroft and an interesting harbour. Between the two, the walk climbs the lovely valley of the River Glaven to reach the village of Glandford, with its ford and unusual Shell Museum near the church.

Cley and its stunning 19th century windmill are the subject of many picture postcards and paintings. Now a quiet backwater (except for the main road in summer), it was once an important port on a huge estuary that filled the Glaven Valley as far as Wiveton. The large and magnificent St Margaret's church, with its 13th century tower, is testimony to this. Look out for several interesting properties in the main street including the old Custom House, built in 1680 and refronted in 1729, and Whalebone House, decorated with sheep vertebrae. Between the village and the sea, the marshes are home to an important bird reserve run by the Norfolk Wildlife Trust.

Glandford is a delightful model village with a picturesque ford through the River Glaven. The Dutch gabled Shell Museum was built in 1915. Nearby, St Martin's church of 1900 was built on the site of an earlier church by Sir Alfred Jodrell of nearby Bayfield Hall in memory of his mother.

The long shingle spit of Blakeney Point (National Trust) shelters the village of Blakeney and its harbour at the end of the New Cut. A popular holiday spot, Blakeney is a huddle of brick and flint houses and cottages lining two lanes leading down to the quay. Here stands the 13th century undercroft of the old guildhall. The hillside behind is dominated by the 15th century west tower of St Nicholas' church with its 13th century chancel. It has a turret which was probably used as a beacon to guide shipping into the port.

Cley's 19th century windmill

The George, a bird watcher's mecca, with its bible containing news of bird sightings and events in the middle bar, is housed in an Edwardian building. It offers hotel accommodation (12 rooms, most with beautiful marsh views) and is a lovely place in which to linger. Nearby is the wildlife haven of Cley Marshes – the first acquisition of the Norfolk Naturalists' (now Wildlife) Trust which was founded in the George in 1926.

Thirsty birdwatchers can partake of Greene King Abbott or Woodforde's real ales. Carlsberg and Stella Artois lagers and Strongbow cider are on draught, together with Guinness. There are separate lunch and dinner menus which are wide ranging and imaginative. For lunch, as well as sandwiches and different jacket potatoes, there are more sophisticated things such as oven baked Cromer crab scented with ginger and lime and glazed with grated cheddar cheese, or slow braised lamb casserole in a rich St Emillion sauce. Dinner could be feuillete filled with fruits of the Norfolk coast enrobed in a light crab bisque. There is a roast on Sundays. Prices are reasonable for this sort of food. There is a good range of vegetarian meals as well. The puddings include locally made ice-cream, sorbet, and home-made fruit crumble.

The rooms are non-smoking except in the village bar and there is a pretty garden over the road for al fresco eating. The George is open all day in summer from 11 am to 11 pm (10.30 pm on Sunday). Lunches are served from 12 noon to 2.30 pm and dinners from 6.30 pm to 9.30 pm. Hours may vary in winter so it is worth checking. Telephone: 01263 740652.

- **How to get there:** Cley-next-the-Sea is on the A149 coast road between Blakeney and Salthouse and the pub is in the centre of the village on a bend soon after the main road swings sharply left.
- **Parking:** There is parking behind the inn. More parking is available at the village hall (see map) or on Blakeney hard (free for National Trust members).
- **Length of the walk:** 7½ miles (with several opportunities for short cuts). Map: OS Explorer 251 Norfolk Coast Central (GR 045439).

The Walk

1. Leave the pub and turn left along the narrow main road. Look for a small flower-decked alleyway next to Whalebone House and turn left up it eventually passing between flint walls to a lane. Turn right. Next on the left is the village hall with parking behind. A small lane goes to the

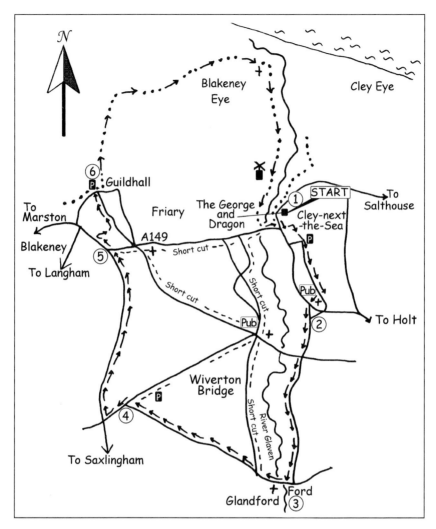

right, but carry on ahead along Church Lane. Where the lane begins to narrow turn right just before a house called The Knoll along a path signposted to St Margaret's church. The church of St Margaret of Antioch is magnificent, a testimony to the wealth that once endowed this former port. Go through a gate into the churchyard and follow the path round to exit via a gate onto Newgate Green. The Three Swallows pub is a little way to the right.

2. Ignore the road to Holt going off to the left and cross the triangle of

The splendid church of St Mary of Antioch, Cley

the green to take the next lane left going to Wiveton and Glandford. The road passes houses and then curves round to a crossroads. (For a short cut, turn right over Wiveton bridge and right again in Wiveton to follow lanes down to the main A149 road where a right turn will bring you back to Cley.) For the main walk, go straight over the crossroads and follow a pretty lane hung with greenery on either side. At the next road junction bear right to the ford and footbridge over the Glaven.

3. Cross the footbridge and continue up the lane ahead lined with Dutch gabled cottages. Glandford church stands on a slope behind them with the Shell Museum in a small building which harmonises with the cottages. At the next crossroads a right turn offers a short cut back to Wiveton and Cley, but for the main walk, take the lane ahead signposted to Langham. Ignore a bridleway on the left which leads to the Bayfield Estate walks. At a road junction, a right turn leads to Wiveton Downs picnic area, then on down to Wiveton providing a short cut.

4. For the main walk, turn left for a short distance and then at a crossroads go right to Blakeney. Walk along this lane ignoring the broad track to the left signposted to Blakeney and continue on down Saxlingham road. The road goes down hill bending slightly to the right and passing a few dwellings to enter Blakeney by a pinewood. Ignore a track to the left between houses and carry on to the main road.

5. Walk to the left here along the pavement and just before a kink in the road cross carefully and take a right turn down Little Lane. Carry on ahead past drives to houses, then along a narrow path between high cobbled walls. Turn left into the High Street which leads down to the quay. At the bottom of the hill to the right is the 13th-century guildhall undercroft.

6. Walk along the sea wall to the right of the Blakeney hard alongside Blakeney channel. Follow the bank round Blakeney Freshes; it veers to the right near Blakeney Eye. At the corner of a barbed wire fence turn right to continue along the sea wall directly towards Cley windmill. Just here are a few flint remains of 13th century Blakeney chapel. The bank veers right and left and then meets a broad crosstrack with a bank ahead. Go up onto the bank. Turn right along the bank which swings round to approach the main A149 coast road. Bear left along the bank parallel to the road and cross over sluice gates on the Glaven then descend down steps (arrow marker) onto the road. Turn left along the road, then left at a road junction back to the pub.

THE NORFOLK COAST PATH – Cley to Salthouse (2 miles)

Turn left off the road some way before the pub opposite a red telephone box. Go down a path behind sea defences leading past Cley windmill on the left and then up onto a grassy bank through marshes, heading with a few changes of direction for the sea. A lane on the right leads in the same direction to the coastguard lookout. Turn right and walk along the beach or take the inland track below the shingle bank which borders Cley Marshes Reserve. The next stage of the walk from Salthouse is reached after just over half a mile.

SALTHOUSE, WALSEY HILLS, SALTHOUSE MARSHES AND THE QUAG

The Dun Cow

If you love miles of empty beach and only the noise of seabirds and the crashing of waves on shingle, this is the walk for you. The wide open spaces of the marsh and sea are in total contrast to the hilly hinterland of farmland and heath behind Salthouse. Wading and water birds abound in the pools and drains of the marshes.

People were making salt at Salthouse at least from medieval and probably from Saxon times, and there is evidence of earlier settlement in the barrows and earthworks on Salthouse Heath above the village. Until the 17th century the village had quays along the line of the main

Salthouse church is set high on the hillside

road. The magnificent 15th century church of St Nicholas, with its interesting graffiti of ships, is set high on a hillside as a beacon to shipping and out of the reach of any flooding of the marshes below.

The Coast Path runs behind the huge shingle bank which acts as a barrier to the sea. It is possible to walk along the beach, but the shingle is tiring to the feet. There is a path behind the bank overlooking several reserves in the pools and marshes behind the bank.

The Dun Cow could not be in a better position. As well as the beer garden there are tables in the sheltered courtyard and a garden area for children. The main building is about 400 years old and was undoubtedly a haunt for smugglers in days gone by when the Salthouse channel flowed past into the Glaven estuary. The pub has one large main room, with 17th century beams and flint walls. There is also a separate non-smoking games bar and two self-catering flats.

The menu offers a choice of sandwiches, salads and beefburgers, with a selection of typical pub hot meals plus a specials board. In addition there are jacket potatoes with a variety of fillings, and a children's menu. Real ales are Tetley Smooth, Greene King Abbot and IPA, as well as Adnam's Broadside. Three lagers are on draught: Carlsberg, Foster's and Stella Artois. The draught cider is Scrumpy Jack

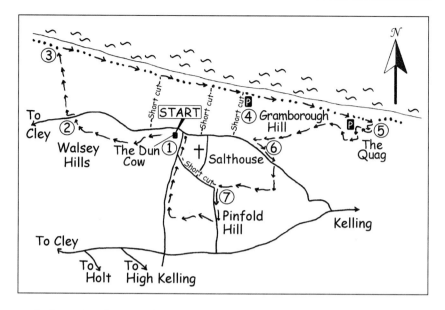

and there is the usual range of other beers including a mild and Guinness. The pub is open all year round from 11 am to 11 pm (10.30 pm on Sunday). Food is served at all reasonable times within those hours. Telephone: 01263 740467.

- **How to get there**: The Dun Cow is on the main A149 coast road at the western end of the village of Salthouse which is between Cley-next-the-Sea and Weybourne.
- **Parking:** In the yard in front of the pub or on the green outside. There is also a car park at the eastern end of Cley Marsh Reserve on the route of this walk and at Kelling Hard.
- **Length of the walk:** 7¼ miles (with several opportunities for short cuts). Map: OS Explorer 251 Norfolk Coast Central (GR 073439).

The Walk

1. Turn right out of the pub and go right again up a lane leading away from the sea. Almost immediately there is a wooden footpath signpost pointing right to Walsey Hills. Cross a stile and cut through between garden and house walls. Go over another stile into a small field and continue on with a wire fence on the right. Cross another stile and go up a wide track through crops. At the end of the field continue on into the rough area of Sarbury Hill. Go over another stile and down a steep

113

slope on the other side. The path forks; take the left branch and go over a stile into another arable field with the route of the path cleared through the middle bearing slightly to the left. At the end of this field go through a hedgerow and carry on ahead again through crops. Go into the next section of field and continue on with a vestigial hedgerow on the left. Where a hedgerow comes in on the left continue on into the next field once more walking through crops. The path goes downhill towards a wooden signpost on a cross track. Turn right along a path which meanders gently through some woodland ignoring paths off. Pass steps leading up to a watch point on Walsey Hills on the right and come to the main road.

2. Cross and turn left along this for a short distance along the raised verge. Turn right off the road at a signpost pointing to the Coast Path and walk along the bank towards the huge wall of pebbles which lines the seashore beyond.

3. The line of the Coast Path here is undefined. One choice is to climb up the shingle bank and turn right along the beach which shelves steeply. Avoid walking on top of the bank which might damage it. An alternative is to walk on the other side of the shingle ridge with the marshes on the right. There is usually a clear track along here unless storms have moved the shingle onto it. If you get tired of walking on the beach there are various short cuts back to Salthouse down tracks through the grazing marshes but only take the obvious ones or you may get cut off by creeks and channels.

After about 15 minutes' steady walking you should find a track behind the shingle leading inland, over the main road and back onto Sarbury Hill where you turn left to return to the village. Another five to ten minutes should bring you opposite another track in line with Salthouse church. Another five minutes and the Beach Road brings you back to the village where a right turn along the main road takes you to the pub.

4. For the full walk continue on along the beach for about another 15 minutes passing the sandy cliff of Gramborough Hill where sand martins nest, to cross the shingle to reach Kelling Hard (parking). The Coast Path continues on here where the land rises below Muckleborough Hill.

5. Here a broad lane leads away from the sea and the Coast Path,

The wonderful interior of St Nicholas's church

zigzagging through the Quag (an NOA bird reserve) with a mere on the left. The lane reaches a cross track. Turn right along this bearing back almost in the direction from which you have come with the shingle bank on the right. This track (Meadow Lane) gradually veers away from the shingle towards Salthouse. The lane eventually reaches the main road where a right turn is a further short cut back to the village.

6. To complete the full walk on the heath above Salthouse, turn left here and walk carefully along the main road for about 100 yards and then just before the road takes a sharp right-hand bend, turn right up a broad unsigned track hedged on both sides. Follow the track (Pinfold Lane) to the right when the way ahead disappears into crops, and pass through folds in the hills. The track goes uphill to meet a metalled lane on a bend. For another short cut back to the village go straight ahead up the lane.

7. For a walk on the heath, turn left along the tiny lane with a big hedge on the right. Pass the track leading up Pinfold Hill on the left, then on the brow of the hill at a wooden footpath signpost, turn right onto the heath, then almost immediately take a right hand branch of the track. Then at the next branching of paths, bear left and follow the wide track through the heath for some distance ignoring a cross track and all smaller side paths.

Remains of wartime brick buildings stand over on the right. The track bends to right and left and comes to a wide parking area. Go ahead onto a metalled cross track then turn left to meet the road. Turn right down the road (Bard Hill) which passes through the heath. Pass a 'road narrows' sign and come gently downhill into Salthouse. Ignore Market Lane going off to the right, continue on down to pass the path taken on the outward journey and carry on to the main road turning left back to the pub.

 THE NORFOLK COAST PATH – Kelling Hard to Sheringham (4 miles)

From Kelling Hard go through a gateway and continue on along the Coast Path alongside the shingle beach with low cliffs on the right. After Beach Lane leading to Weybourne Hope, the path goes up onto the cliffs and veers round a house and wall returning to the cliffs and heading for Sheringham. Take care as the cliffs are very crumbly. Carry on alongside a golf course, then climb Skelding Hill passing the coastguard station. Walk down into Sheringham and continue ahead along the promenade to meet the next walk.

SHERINGHAM, BEESTON REGIS HEATH AND BEESTON PRIORY
The Windham Arms

This walk offers the chance, rare in Norfolk, to tackle some fairly steep climbs and to enjoy excellent views as your reward. From Beeston Bump there are views along the coast or inland through trees to Augustinian Beeston priory which can be explored on the return journey. Inland the walk passes through a small section of Beeston Heath to come back through the byways of old Sheringham via interesting little lokes, and commons bisected by a stream.

When the railway came to Sheringham, the town developed as a popular seaside resort. Now the station is also the terminus for the North Norfolk Railway's Poppy Line steam railway which runs to Weybourne and Holt. The little flint-built village of Upper Sheringham on the hillside used to be more important than its fishing village neighbour by the sea. Now its claim to fame is beautiful Sheringham Park owned by the National Trust.

The village of Beeston which now joins on to Sheringham was an important stop on the pilgrimage to Walsingham. Its early 13th century Augustinian priory is now a picturesque ruin. The nearby church of All Saints stands forlorn amidst caravans. Parts of Beeston Regis heath are owned by the National Trust as is adjoining Roman Camp, where Beacon Hill is the highest point in the county.

The Windham Arms is a friendly pub, popular with residents and holidaymakers alike. It is well-known locally for its range of real ales. On offer are Woodforde's Wherry, Adnam's bitter and Broadside, Buckley's Best and a changing guest ale, though there could well be more in summer. Strongbow cider is on draught as are Foster's and Kronenbourg lagers. There is a typical pub menu, with fish and chips and pies, as well as burgers, baguettes, panini and jacket potatoes. There is a specials board, with an emphasis on fish in season, and dishes such as chicken with cashew and oyster sauce. There are at least three vegetarian choices as well as a children's menu and a large choice of puddings. There is a children's room at the back of the building. An area of the restaurant is non-smoking. There is also a Shanty bar and tables outside in summer.

Opening hours Monday to Saturday are from 11 am to 11 pm; Sundays from 12 noon to 10.30 pm. Food is served from 12 noon to 2 pm and from 6 pm to 9 pm (slightly later on Sundays). Telephone: 01263 822609.

- **HOW TO GET THERE**: Sheringham is on the A149 coast road between Weybourne and Cromer. The pub is in Windham Street, off the High Street, and set just back from the promenade.
- **PARKING:** In the pub car park, approached via a slip road to the right just after Windham Street off High Street. Alternative parking can be found near the start of the walk in a public car park off Beeston Road, which is the first main turn left after the roundabout going out of Sheringham in the Cromer direction.
- **LENGTH OF THE WALK:** 3½ miles (which could be extended by following the walks on Beeston Heath). Map: Explorer 252 Norfolk Coast East (GR 159435).

THE WALK

1. Come out to the back of the pub and walk past the Crown to the sea

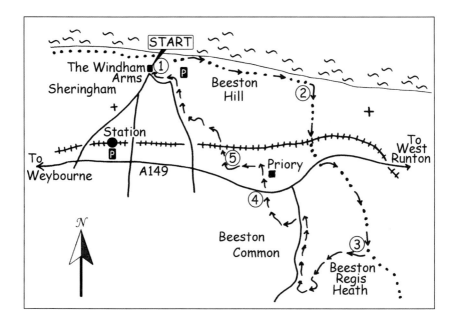

front. Turn right along the promenade, go down steps to the right and then carry on again.

Follow the promenade, which is now the route of the Coast Path, round to the right. Cross a boat launching ramp bearing left and carry on along the east promenade looking out over beaches and breakwaters. Pass Shannock ice cream parlour beside which are steps leading up to a public car park (mentioned under Parking above). A little further on the Coast Path is signposted up steps to the right by toilets. It then goes up a broad concrete track between grassy banks. Turn left at the top (signpost), pass a putting green on the left and carry on along a stony track curving round to the right. Go through a metal barrier and later where the path branches, take the left fork and go up Beeston Hill. Keep clear of the crumbling cliff. Go downhill, again with steps to help, and continue along the cliff top as far as the camping field.

2. Turn right keeping a fence on the left and walk to the level crossing. Trains leave Sheringham for Cromer and Norwich so take care in crossing. Continue ahead down a wide stony lane to the main road (signpost). Cross carefully, turn left along the pavement for a very short distance and then turn almost immediately half right through a wooden gate (signposted to Roman Camp). Bear right along the broad track near

The ruins of Beeston Regis priory

a row of flint cottages, then pass Beeston Hall School on the left and attractive flint Hall Farm. The track continues on through fields rising up towards woods where it meets a cross track at a National Trust (Beeston Regis Heath) sign. The Coast Path goes to the left.

3. This walk goes ahead here into the woods along a narrow track signposted with a National Trust walks sign. This bears right and runs parallel with the broader track on the edge of the woods below. At a junction of paths turn right off the more main track and continue on along this narrow track. Cross over a broad cross track, climb a steep hill. Turn right at a broad cross track to meet the lane. Turn left at this lane to a house near a National Trust sign. Turn right down the lane to a road (signpost). Turn right down the road walking along the pavement on the right soon passing houses. Cross Regis Avenue and continue on. Cross the road and turn into the modern housing estate of Priory Close. Turn right where it says Nos 16-19 and 51-56. Turn right along a tarmacked footpath by the side of No 13, bear left through metal barriers then turn right along another estate road. Take the turning leading to Nos 57-64 and follow the road round bearing left. Go down

On the Coast Path between Weybourne and Sheringham

another footpath passing the garage of No 64 on the right. This bears round to the right with a pleasant common area on the left. Go through metal railings to the main road.

4. Turn right then shortly cross and go left down a broad stony track (signpost) passing between a private garden and a private drive. Pass the cobbled wall of a house and come to the magnificent ruins of Beeston Regis Priory. It was founded in 1216 for four canons and closed by Henry VIII in 1540. Go out by a wooden gate, then follow the direction of a footpath signpost which points left to a road. Pass some old cottages, then take a slip road to the right, passing more cottages on the right and a tiny Gothic cobbled cottage on the left. Where the road bends left, go straight ahead on a causeway alongside a little stream. Continue into a rough common area. Bear right along the hard path which goes over the stream. The path goes through railings and onto a road.

5. Turn right under the railway bridge to another green, edged with houses. Turn left along the path, still following the stream. Go through railings and continue on along the back of houses on a broader track (Back Loke). The stream crosses to the right. Come out onto Priory

Road and turn left to its junction with Beeston Road turning right. Cross over a turning to the right and then two more to the left. The next right turn leads to the public car park mentioned under Parking (above). There is a little slip lane going straight ahead but bear left down Windham Street and back to the pub.

 THE NORFOLK COAST PATH - Beeston Regis Heath to Roman Camp (1¼ miles)

From the National Trust sign at Beeston Regis Heath, the Coast Path bears left along a track called Calves Well Lane, soon leaving this track to bear right through woods towards Roman Camp near Beacon Hill (346 ft), the highest point in Norfolk. The track passes Roman Camp caravan site and comes out onto a road.

CROMER AND FELBRIGG HALL

The Old Red Lion

This walk leaves Cromer with its reminders of former Edwardian seaside delights to follow the first part of the Weaver's Way (a 56 mile walking route between Cromer and Great Yarmouth) to Jacobean Felbrigg Hall. A delightful walk through the park and woods of this National Trust property leads towards the Coast Path, which here runs through high wooded ground a mile or so from the seashore back into Cromer, finishing at the famous pier.

Originally a fishing village, Cromer developed as a fashionable seaside resort with the arrival of the railway in Victorian times. Smart people continued to flock to the resort in Edwardian times because the area had been popularised as 'Poppyland' by journalist Clement Scott. The imposing church of St Peter and St Paul has a magnificent west tower, the tallest in Norfolk. It was magnificently restored by Blomfield in the

1880s. Cromer museum, near the church, is housed in a row of fishermen's cottages whereas the Lifeboat museum is in the Old Boathouse – Cromer's lifeboats have had a heroic history. Fishing boats still go out to catch the famous Cromer crabs. The pier was built in 1900. Just outside the town but on the route of this walk is Gothic Cromer Hall, built of flint in 1829.

It is a treat to be able to walk through the beautiful grounds of Felbrigg Hall (National Trust). The Hall dates from Jacobean times, with later alterations, and the fine castellated stable yard was built in 1825. It has an exquisite walled garden, with an eye-catching brick dovecote. The church of St Margaret of Antioch was rebuilt in the 15th century and has splendid Wyndham family monuments. Felbrigg's Great Wood (an SSSI) is nationally important for fungi and lichens.

The Old Red Lion is a Victorian hotel that boasts one of the finest positions on the Norfolk coast. It stands tall on a cliff corner, its oriel windows in a fanciful tower looking out onto the pier. Below it, steps lead steeply to the beach not far from where the fishing boats are drawn up in front of the lifeboat station. The cosy bars looking out onto the sea have an Edwardian atmosphere with mahogany fittings, salt glaze pottery, old bottles and pewter mugs. Freehold and family run, the hotel has twelve bedrooms and is open all day from 10 am to 11 pm providing a haven of comfort with good sustaining food and drink whatever the weather. There is an attractive conservatory at the back.

The hotel restaurant, Galliano's, opens at 6.30 pm in the evening and offers an extensive à la carte as well as a tempting table d' hôte menu. There are various vegetarian options. The menus change regularly according to season. Food is served from 12 noon to 2.30 pm and from 6 pm to 9.45 pm. There is something for everyone from sandwiches to steaks. Children are welcome and have their own section of the menu. Morning coffee and cream teas are also served. The well-kept real ales include Abbot and Adnam's with a regularly changing guest beer which could be something like Old Speckled Hen. Strongbow is the draught cider and a wide selection of other beers and lagers is available. Dogs are not allowed. Telephone: 01263 514964.

- **How to get there:** Come in on the A148 from Holt following signs to Cromer town centre. The Meadow car park is on the right. For the Red Lion, continue on turning right into Church Street. Go past the church and turn left into Brook Street, then right into the hotel car park.
- **Parking:** The hotel car park or The Meadow car park (see above) which

is the start of Weaver's Way and the Norfolk Coast Path. There is also parking at Felbrigg Hall.
- **LENGTH OF THE WALK:** 6¾ miles. Map OS Explorer 252 Norfolk Coast East (GR 221423).

THE WALK

1. Leave the Red Lion turning left. Ignore the first turn left, which leads to the hotel car park, and continue on along Tucker Street to the 15th-century church of St Peter and St Paul which has the tallest spire in Norfolk. Just before the church, turn left through the churchyard passing delightful Cromer museum housed in a row of fishermen's cottages. Turn right into Church Street, a major thoroughfare of shops and offices, and continue along it passing the parish hall on the left.

After this take the first turn on the left (Chapel Street) to cross a main road and reach The Meadow car park leading onto a green recreation area beyond. From the car park, bear right across the recreation area or walk along Meadow Road on the right, then bear left into Hall Road. Cromer is soon left behind as the walk leaves the 30 mph limit and passes a little gatehouse on the right. A Weaver's Way signpost points back across The Meadow and up the road which has a small pavement on the left and passes through a pleasant stretch of woodland. Continue past the imposing gates leading to Gothic Cromer Hall. When the pavement ends, carry on ahead along the road passing another lodge and entrance to Cromer Hall.

Soon after tile-hung Home Farm Lodge, Weaver's Way is signposted by an arrow marker on a wooden signpost pointing half right through the middle of a field. A farm track sweeps up to the left. The track passes along the edge of a tree-studded knoll. The delightful wooded scenery and poppy-strewn fields are a reminder of the name 'Poppyland', when the area was made famous by the writings of Victorian Clement Scott. Another arrow on a post points the way through the field, and on towards a red brick bridge over a single track railway. The farm track approaches the bridge on the left (arrow markers).

2. Cross the bridge, ignore the wide track sweeping right and carry straight ahead along a narrow signposted track between the edge of a field and some back gardens. Follow the path as it zigzags round the edge of the field. Ignore a narrow path which goes left through woods and carry on a little further to where the path goes left down some steps to a little lane. Leave the Weaver's Way (which goes up steps and on

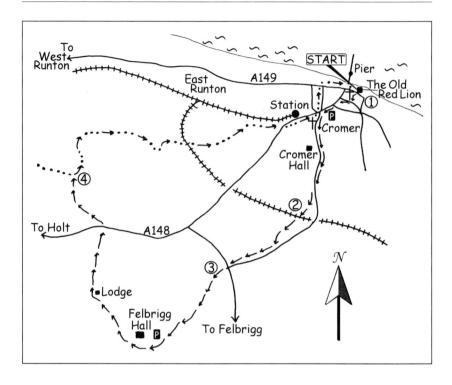

through woodland on the left) here, and carry on up the lane which passes through more woods to reach a T-junction with the B1436 opposite the entrance to historic Felbrigg Hall with its lake, medieval church, and beautiful garden. The National Trust allow access to walkers every day from dawn until dusk except Christmas Day.

3. Cross the road and go through between charming little gatehouses embellished with coats of arms. Carry on down the drive through rhododendron woods and an avenue of oak trees. Go over several cattle grids with pedestrian gates keeping on the main drive and enjoying the views over the park and church. Carry on through the car parking area, and follow the drive as it sweeps round the house. Continue on the drive away from the Hall and over another cattle grid passing a picnic area on the right. Continue on to Sexton's Gate with its pretty lodge to meet a tiny lane.

Turn right and follow the lane's gentle curves downhill through woodland (the Lion's Mouth). Take care as cars leave the Hall along this route. The lane bears right to meet the A148 road. Take a short cut up the bank as the lane bears right. Cross the road carefully, walking a short

Cromer pier

way to the left to turn off right down another wooded lane (no right turn for traffic here) with houses on the left. Pass a water tower on the right. Continue on past a left turn until you come to a crossing of wide tracks which is the route of the Coast Path.

4. Turn right past a wide area for parking. At a wooden signpost pointing straight ahead, bear left down a broad stony track (arrow marker on a low post on the right). This sunken path curves on gently for some distance with rhododendron woods banked quite steeply on either side. Ignore a signpost to the left and follow the main track round to the right.

Near the entrance to a large camping site (signpost) the route narrows, skirting along the edge of the camping ground for some distance to meet a crossroads of tracks at a signpost. Keep on ahead along a narrow path. Then pass through woodland and go through a kissing-gate into farmland. Go through a second kissing gate and over a little bridge and continue on over Abbs Common to a broad cross track. Go ahead by a grassy triangle on the left to another broad branch of the track. Bear right here at a wooden signpost along a broad path (Cross

127

Lane) which then narrows down tunnel-like between hedges.

The track opens out where two fields join and immediately continues on ahead again in a tunnel of trees. Now the track comes out near housing and joins a wider farm track. Carry straight on, then, where the farm track goes off to the right, keep on ahead with Manor Farm on the left to cross a tiny lane (signpost) and reach a railway bridge. Go under this along a broad stony track (Newstead Lane) with camping fields on either side.

The track climbs a hill, then begins its descent in the direction of Cromer church tower. Cross a road leading to works on the left and go on ahead along a small roadway (arrow marker) through workshops. Ignore a road going off to the left. Then the road becomes Sandy Lane and passes through housing to emerge on the Holt road (A148). Continue down this passing the station on the left to cross over at a crossroads to a road called The Meadow bearing right to The Meadow car park and the terminus of the Coast Path. From here retrace your steps to the Red Lion.

 ### THE NORFOLK COAST PATH FINALE (¼ mile)

Cromer pier would seem to be a better terminus for such a varied and glorious Long Distance Route, so for a finish with a flourish, turn left up Beach Road soon after the station and carry on over two junctions, passing a car park with toilets on the right, to the main Runton Road (A149). Bear right along the cliffs passing a sunken garden and keep following the cliff top path eventually zigzagging down a path to reach Cromer pier. From here you continue on past the Bath House pub and climb steps back up to the Red Lion.